HEALING YOUR
GRIEVING HEART
AFTER MISCARRIAGE

*Companion Press is dedicated to the education
and support of both the bereaved and bereavement
caregivers. We believe that those who companion
the bereaved by walking with them as they journey
in grief have a wondrous opportunity: to help others
embrace and grow through grief—and to lead
fuller, more deeply-lived lives themselves
because of this important ministry.*

Companion
PRESS

For a complete catalog and ordering information, write or call:

Companion Press
The Center for Loss and Life Transition
3735 Broken Bow Road
Fort Collins, CO 80526
(970) 226-6050
www.centerforloss.com

HEALING YOUR
GRIEVING HEART
AFTER MISCARRIAGE

•

100 PRACTICAL IDEAS
FOR PARENTS AND FAMILIES

•

ALAN D. WOLFELT, PH.D.

Companion
P R E S S

Fort Collins, Colorado
An imprint of the Center for Loss and Life Transition

Companion Press is an imprint of the Center for Loss and Life Transition, 3735 Broken Bow Road, Fort Collins, Colorado 80526.

23 22 21   5 4 3

ISBN: 978-1-61722-218-4

In Gratitude

*To the parents who have allowed me to companion them
in the aftermath of miscarriage and all other forms
of early pregnancy loss. You have enriched my life
and inspired me to pen this resource. Thank you for
teaching me what it means to love and hope.*

CONTENTS

INTRODUCTION

I'd like to begin by affirming an important truth: Miscarriage is a significant loss.

It is normal and natural to hurt deeply after miscarriage, and I am truly sorry for your loss.

While sometimes others will imply or outright tell you that miscarriage happens too early on for you to be attached to the baby, that miscarriage is so common it's nothing to get upset about, or that you should focus on getting pregnant again instead of being sad about what happened, *you* know that miscarriage and ectopic pregnancy often feel like profound losses to the women who experience them as well as to their partners and others who are close to them.

Your grief is real. Your grief is justified. And the depth of your grief has less to do with the number of weeks that you were pregnant and more to do with the attachment you felt to this developing baby or the idea of your future with a child. The more you wanted this baby, the more invested you were in your hopes and dreams for a child, the more painful your grief journey will likely be.

Love plus loss equals grief. If you wanted and loved this baby, of course you grieve. And now you must mourn. The purpose of this book is to help you mourn and heal.

Even though I have been a grief counselor and educator for almost 40 years, I cannot fully understand what you are feeling. I am a father with three children, and I have counseled couples and families after pregnancy loss, but I do not have personal experience with miscarriage. And while I have already written a 100 Ideas book for families who have suffered stillbirth, I know that miscarriage grief is unique in some ways. To help me better attune to your unique experience, I turned to Lori-Ann Huot, Program Coordinator for the Angel Whispers Baby Loss Support Program in Alberta, Canada, which supports parents who have lost a baby during pregnancy or shortly after birth.

Thank you to Lori-Ann for sharing her thoughts with me about miscarriage, molar pregnancy, and ectopic pregnancy.

Miscarriage, ectopic pregnancy, and other early pregnancy loss

It's thought that as many as half of all pregnancies end in miscarriage—many before the woman even knows that one of her eggs has been fertilized and before she has missed a period. Among women who know they are pregnant, the miscarriage rate is about 15 percent. This makes miscarriage an extraordinarily prevalent form of loss—one thought to affect about a million couples each year in the United States alone.

The March of Dimes defines miscarriage as "when a baby dies in the womb before 20 weeks of pregnancy." That means that the term "miscarriage" covers a wide range of pregnancy loss experiences. As you probably know, early miscarriage, which is by far the most common, is considered pregnancy loss before 12 weeks' gestation, and late miscarriage covers the time period from 12 weeks to 19 ⅞ weeks' gestation. Beginning at 20 weeks, pregnancy loss is called stillbirth. In addition to these medical-world parameters and terms, early pregnancy loss also includes molar pregnancy and ectopic pregnancy as well as blighted ovum, each of which has its own unique clinical definitions and causes.

If you (or someone in your family) suffered any of these kinds of pregnancy loss, this book is for you. I realize that the different types and stages of miscarriage can result in markedly different pregnancy-loss experiences for women. Late miscarriage, for example, may end with the mother delivering a baby in the hospital, while in early miscarriage (or ectopic pregnancy) there is often no baby to see. Still, for the most part what we will be focusing on in the pages to come is the emotional and spiritual journey that follows miscarriage of any kind—and that journey is shaped more by the depth of the love and attachment than it is by weeks' gestation or clinical terminology and diagnoses.

That is not to say that everyone who has miscarried has the same grief experience. That would be like assuming that everyone who has lived through the death of a grandparent suffers the same grief. Of course not! Grief is never the same twice. Every grief journey is as unique as the two people who were bound by love and then separated by death.

Yet families who share the same type of loss—in this case, miscarriage—have much in common. In this book I seek to find that common ground and offer affirmation and support.

The time betwixt and between

One of the main ways in which the grief following miscarriage is unlike any other has to do with early pregnancy's mystery. Early pregnancy may appear as a plus sign on a home pregnancy test, but other than that, it is often invisible.

In the first few days after an egg is fertilized, life is forming on the cellular level. It is microscopically tiny, and it is also hidden from view. Once the cells (called the blastocyst at this point) embed in the lining of the uterus, the medical field calls the baby not a baby but an embryo. By the end of week five, the healthy embryo is only ¼-inch long and does not look human, though he or she has a beating heart. By the end of week eight, the embryo is one inch long and doctors start to call him or her a fetus.

Most miscarriages happen in these early weeks. This is what I would call the "liminal" period of life. Liminal means a transitional stage or a threshold—the time betwixt and between. From a strictly biological standpoint, the embryo, or fetus, is alive, but he or she is not developed enough to really look like a baby, be known as a boy or a girl, be born, or survive.

With very late miscarriage and stillbirth, a baby emerges. But with most miscarriages, there is pregnancy and then no pregnancy. Oh yes, there is still love and attachment—we have already established and strongly affirmed that. But there will be no baby to hold and bury, no footprints to ink onto paper, no locks of hair to save, no photos to cherish.

The mystery, invisibility, and liminal quality of miscarriage makes it unique among significant losses. Your love for this baby—or, for some couples in early pregnancy, what may be more accurately described as your desire for a baby— was very real, but having nothing tangible to hold onto can make your loss seem that much more devastating and, in some ways, *un*real.

What's more, the words we use to describe miscarriage only reinforce its amorphous qualities. First of all, the term "miscarriage" can be understood as implying fault on the part of the mother, as if she didn't carry the baby well enough. The word itself is part of the problem, yet it is the best we have. Similarly, "embryo" and "fetus" may be technically correct, but they don't capture the love and loss you feel. The word "baby" may or may not seem right to you, either. Some families who experience early miscarriage feel that what they have lost is not so much a baby as a feeling of hope and possibility for a child. Yet I will use the word "baby" throughout this book because I believe it is the best and most loving alternative. (See Idea 3 for more on using the words that feel right to *you*.)

So if you are feeling that your loss is not understood or recognized in our culture, or that you yourself feel unsure about what you have lost or how to talk about it, you are not alone. Rest assured, however, that the mystery, invisibility, and liminality of miscarriage do not *at all* mean that your loss is insignificant. These qualities just make it harder to talk about. In fact, the English language and Western ways of thinking about early pregnancy seem to collude in marginalizing and disenfranchising your grief. I hope this book will help all of us find ways to talk about, recognize, and support miscarriage grief.

Grief and mourning after miscarriage

Grief is what we think and feel inside ourselves after a significant loss. Mourning is the expression of those thoughts and feelings. Everyone who suffers loss experiences grief, but if you are to heal, you must also mourn. Another term you may encounter after loss is "bereaved," which literally means "to be torn apart" and "to have special needs."

Yes, you've been torn apart by this loss, and you have special needs that must be tended to in the weeks, months, and years to come. Perhaps your most important special need right now is to be compassionate with yourself. The word "compassion" literally means "with passion." So, self-compassion means caring for yourself with passion. While I hope you have excellent outside support, this little book is intended to help you be kind to and patient with yourself as you acknowledge and eventually embrace your grief over the loss of this baby.

Over my years of walking with people in grief, I have discovered that many of us are hard on ourselves when we are in mourning. We often have inappropriate expectations of how "well" we should be doing with our grief. These expectations result from common societal messages that tell us to be strong in the face of grief. We are told to "carry on," "keep your chin up," and "keep busy." This is especially true in the aftermath of inappropriately minimized losses like miscarriage. In actuality, when we are in grief we need to slow down, turn inward, embrace and express our feelings of loss, and seek and accept support. It's not easy to be self-compassionate in our mourning-avoiding culture.

But good self-care is essential to your survival. To practice good self-care doesn't mean you are feeling sorry for yourself; rather, it means you are helping yourself to heal. For it is in nurturing ourselves, in allowing ourselves the time and loving attention we need to journey through our grief, that we find meaning in our continued living. It is in having the courage to care for our own needs that we discover a fullness to living and loving again.

I hope the words I express from my heart to yours throughout the following pages bring you some solace. Of course, I realize that no book can take your overwhelming loss away. It rages in the recesses of your soul. Your profound loss will endure, and nothing I can say or do will alter that truth.

Yet I also truly believe that acknowledging your heart is broken is the beginning of your healing. As you experience the pain of your loss—gently opening, acknowledging, and allowing—the suffering it has wrought diminishes but never completely vanishes. In fact, the resistance to the pain can potentially be more painful than the pain itself. Running from the pain of loss closes down our hearts and spirits. As difficult as it is, we must relinquish ourselves to the pain of grief. As Helen Keller said, "The best way out is always through."

Yet going through the pain of loss is not in and of itself the goal in our grief journeys. Instead, it is rediscovering life in ways that give us reason to get our feet out of bed and to make life matter. I'm certain you realize that your loss of this baby is not something you will ever "overcome" or "let go of." Pregnancy loss doesn't call out to be "resolved" or "explained" but to be experienced.

As promised, this book contains 100 practical ideas to help you heal. Some of the ideas will teach you about the principles of grief and mourning. One of the most important ways to help yourself is to learn about the grief experience; the more you know, the less likely you will be to unknowingly perpetuate some of our society's harmful myths about grief and healing.

The remainder of the 100 ideas offer practical, here-and-now, action-oriented tips for embracing your grief. Each idea is followed by a brief explanation of how and why the idea might help you.

You'll also notice that each of the 100 ideas suggests a *carpe diem*, which means, as fans of the movie *Dead Poets Society* will remember, "seize the day." My hope is that you will not relegate this book to your shelves but keep it handy on your nightstand or desk. Pick it up often and turn to any page; the *carpe diem* suggestion will encourage you to seize the day by helping you move toward healing today, right now, right this minute. If you come to an idea that doesn't seem to fit you, simply ignore it and flip to a different page.

May you discover courage in places both obvious and hidden along the way. May you stay present to your grief and be filled with a commitment to see what it has to say. May you hold hope, courage, and faith high like a candle in the dark and bravely walk forward, even when everything inside of you urges you to turn and run away.

Bless you. I hope to meet you one day.

Alan D. Wolfelt

1.

EMBRACE YOUR NEED AND RIGHT TO GRIEVE

"So it's true, when all is said and done, grief is the price we pay for love."
— E. A. Bucchianeri

- No matter what others might wrong-headedly say or imply about the supposed relative inconsequentiality of miscarriage, you *have* suffered a significant loss. Of course you are grieving! Of course you have a need and right to mourn!

- Miscarriage and ectopic pregnancy are *not* negligible losses. Your loss is exactly as profound as it feels to you inside. Your reality is real.

- Still, not everyone whose life has been touched by miscarriage feels the same. Each person's sense of loss and grief is as unique as a snowflake. Your thoughts and feelings will not be the same as your partner's or others grieving the loss of this baby. And you will find that other families who have experienced miscarriage will not necessarily share your precise thoughts and feelings. That's OK. There is no right or wrong. Everyone is entitled to their own unique grief and mourning after a loss.

- Affirm your need and right to mourn. If other people act as if nothing's happened or judge your grief, try to understand that they have been conditioned by a culture that minimizes loss in general and miscarriage in particular. Educate them. And turn to others who *are* able to empathize with your loss.

CARPE DIEM
Today, tell someone about what this miscarriage has meant to you.

2.

MOURN YOUR LOSS

"There is no foot so small that it cannot leave an imprint on this world."
— Unknown

- Everyone grieves when we lose something significant, but if we are to heal our grief, we must also mourn.

- Your body's and mind's natural response to miscarriage is to grieve. Grief is the constellation of internal thoughts and feelings you have when you lose someone you love and value.

- Your grief is what you may feel as a weight in your chest, a churning in your stomach, an ache in your arms, memories of your miscarriage experience, or bittersweet thoughts of a hoped-for future that will never be.

- Mourning, on the other hand, is the outward expression of your grief. It is an active process. Mourning is releasing your grief, be it through crying, writing your thoughts in a journal, creating art that represents your feelings of grief, talking to others about what happened, or participating in a support group.

- Many of the ideas in this book are intended to help you mourn your loss of this baby. These ideas have been written to help you express your grief outside of yourself so that over time your heart can heal.

CARPE DIEM
Check in with yourself and ask, "Am I allowing myself to actively mourn this loss, or am I holding my grief inside?"

3.

USE THE WORDS THAT FEEL RIGHT TO YOU

"Better than a thousand hollow words is one word that brings peace."

— Buddha

- With miscarriage, especially losses in the early weeks of pregnancy, finding the right words to describe your loss can be hard.
- Do you say that you lost a pregnancy? Do you say that your baby died? Do you simply say that you miscarried?
- Many families affected by miscarriage are hurt when they hear doctors use terms like "spontaneous abortion," "products of conception," and "fetal demise." While these words may be medically accurate, they are not compassionate nor do they capture families' profound feelings of love and loss. What's more, the word "miscarriage" may seem to lay blame on the mother for not carrying her child well enough. I actually think that our very lexicon of pregnancy loss needs an overhaul.
- Empower yourself by using the words that best capture your unique thoughts and feelings about your loss. If it feels right to you to use the word "baby," then by all means, do so—regardless of how far along you were in your pregnancy.
- Similarly, work to find words to describe your emotions. When someone asks, "How are you?", perhaps you can honestly say, "I've been feeling really (sad, angry, lonely, lost, or heartbroken)." Or, "This week was really hard for me because…" Saying "I'm fine" or "I'm doing OK" if you're not doesn't serve you or the listener very well.
- Also consider naming the baby you lost. We name people because they are unique, once-in-forever individuals. If you feel this way about the baby who was miscarried, then by all means pick a name so that you have a way to talk about him or her as time passes. Gender-neutral names such as Jessie or Riley might be appropriate, or you could choose a simple term of endearment such as "pumpkin" or "sweet pea."

CARPE DIEM
Talk to your partner or a close friend or family member about
the language you want to use (and just as important,
don't want to use) in talking about your loss.

4.

UNDERSTAND THE SIX NEEDS OF MOURNING

Need 1. Acknowledge the reality of this loss

"Seeing is always an act of courage."
— Marty Rubin

- Your developing baby has died. This is a difficult reality to accept. Your mind and heart may try to push this reality away at first. In the beginning, some degree of denial is normal and necessary for your survival. Yet gently, slowly, and patiently, over time, you must begin to embrace this reality. Little by little. Hour by hour. You will come to integrate the reality in doses as you are ready.

- Acknowledging the full reality of your loss will happen as time passes. Over the coming months and years there will be many experiences that will remind you of this reality. These are necessary experiences for you to have, as painful as they may be.

- You will first acknowledge the reality of your loss with your head, and then, eventually, you will begin to acknowledge the reality with your heart and soul.

CARPE DIEM
Tell someone about your miscarriage today.

5.

UNDERSTAND THE SIX NEEDS
OF MOURNING

Need 2. Embrace the pain of the loss

"We must embrace pain and burn it as fuel for our journey."
— Kenji Miyazawa

- Embracing pain sounds counterintuitive. In fact, you may be actively looking for ways to avoid or prevent yourself from feeling the pain of your miscarriage day in and day out. It is easier to avoid, repress, or push away the pain of grief than it is to confront it and feel through it.

- Yet confronting and allowing your pain to surface is what will help you reconcile and integrate your loss. As I often say, you must feel it to heal it.

- In the early days after your miscarriage, your pain may seem ever-present, as if it doesn't let up for even a moment. Your every thought and feeling may seem to be centered on your loss. While you do need to experience your pain, you can only do so in doses. Take breaks. It's healthy to seek distractions and allow yourself bits of pleasure every day. Go for a walk, watch TV, or talk to friends about something other than the loss.

CARPE DIEM

Dedicate 15 minutes right now to thinking about and feeling your loss.
If you don't want to be alone for this, reach out to someone who
doesn't try to stop your tears or tell you not to hurt. Sit with this person
as you express how painful this experience is for you.

6.

UNDERSTAND THE SIX NEEDS OF MOURNING

Need 3. Remember what happened

"Memory is the diary that we all carry about with us."
— Oscar Wilde

- You experienced a pregnancy and then the loss of a pregnancy. Depending on the number of weeks' gestation and the type of miscarriage, you may or may not have seen the baby on ultrasound (or for later miscarriages, after delivery), listened to the heartbeat, experienced pregnancy symptoms, or felt him or her move inside you. But regardless, from the moment you knew you were pregnant, your life changed. It changed again after your miscarriage.

- Whenever we experience significant loss in life, we hold its memory in our hearts. Loss changes us. And remembering loss is a form of honoring our lives, our reality, and what made us who we are today. To strive *not* to remember, on the other hand, is to dishonor our lives and our reality.

- If those around you try to take memories away from you in a misguided attempt to spare you from more pain, let them know that this is not helpful. It is good for you to talk about the pregnancy and miscarriage. It is good to display ultrasound pictures or cards that people may have sent you, show people the nursery or baby items you'd purchased, and share the hopes and dreams you had for this baby's future.

- Remind yourself that it is remembering the past that makes hoping for the future possible.

CARPE DIEM

If you have mementos from this pregnancy, such as a pregnancy test, a newspaper printed on the day of the miscarriage, ultrasound pictures, photos taken of you when you were pregnant, or a list of names you were considering, gather everything up and place it in a special memory box that you can go through whenever you're thinking about this baby.

7.

UNDERSTAND THE SIX NEEDS
OF MOURNING

Need 4. Develop a new self-identity

*"An identity would seem to be arrived at by the way in which the person
faces and uses his experience."*

— James Baldwin

- A big part of our self-identities are formed by the roles we play in life.
  You were pregnant, about to become a new mother or father. But you
  didn't reach parenthood, at least not for this baby. How does this affect
  your self-identity? Your partner, the baby's grandparents, and the baby's
  siblings (if there are any) will also struggle with how they think of
  themselves and the family in the aftermath of the miscarriage.

- Even if you have other children, this baby's death will probably change
  your self-perception in many ways.

- In the search to better understand why their loss occurred, many
  parents will try to find blame with themselves. Rarely is a miscarriage
  related to something the mother or father has done wrong. Instead,
  the feelings of blame often stem from the fact that our sense of self
  is always, always affected by significant loss—especially when an
  immediate family member dies.

- In the months and years to come, if you mourn fully and honestly, you
  will find ways to accommodate this loss into your sense of self and family.

CARPE DIEM
Work on articulating how this loss is changing you. Complete the
following sentences with the words that feel right to you. I used to be
_____. Since the miscarriage, I am _____.
When I used to think about _____, I felt _____.
Today, when I think about _____, I feel _____.
Keeping writing as long as you want.

8.

UNDERSTAND THE SIX NEEDS
OF MOURNING

Need 5. Search for meaning

"Here is the world. Beautiful and terrible things will happen. Don't be afraid."
— Frederick Buechner

- When a baby dies, it feels so unnatural and out of order. We question the meaning and purpose of this sad turn of events. No question is too small or too strange. All of them are important questions to ask. Why did this child die before me? Why does a baby die before he is even born? What is the point in that?

- "Why" questions may surface uncontrollably and often precede "how" questions. This mental quandary that occurs with grief can feel consuming at times. You might be asking, "Why did this happen? Why me? How will my life be different? How will it be the same?"

- You will likely question your philosophy of life and explore what really matters to you as you work on this mourning need.

- Remember that having faith or spirituality does not eliminate your need to mourn. Even if you believe in an afterlife of some kind, you and this child have still lost precious time together here on Earth. It's normal to feel dumbfounded and angry at God or whatever source within the universe you may believe has permitted this to happen.

- Ultimately, you may decide that there is no answer to the question "Why did this happen?" For some parents the only answer is this: Miscarriage does not make sense and it never will.

CARPE DIEM

Start a list of "why" questions that have surfaced for you since your miscarriage. Find a friend or counselor who will explore (not tritely answer) these questions with you and help you arrive at your own answers over time. Encourage your partner to do the same.

9.

UNDERSTAND THE SIX NEEDS
OF MOURNING

Need 6. Receive ongoing support from others

"You must be at the end of your rope. I felt a tug."

— Unknown

- As mourners we need the love and understanding of others as we move through our grief toward healing.
- Don't feel ashamed by your heightened dependence on others right now. If your miscarriage was recent, you may feel the need to be around people all the time. You might feel compelled to talk about the pregnancy often. You may need help with day-to-day tasks that you have no energy for right now, such as getting meals together, doing laundry, or completing paperwork. Rather than feel bad about this, take comfort in the knowledge that others care about you.
- Unfortunately, our society places too much value on "carrying on" and "doing well" after a loss. So, mourners are often abandoned by their friends and family soon after a loss. This is especially true after miscarriage because many don't appreciate that it is a significant and painful loss. And sometimes family and friends avoid encounters because they don't know what to say.
- Keep in mind the rule of thirds: one third of your friends will be supportive of your need to mourn, one third will make you feel worse, and one third will neither help nor hinder. Identify the first third and spend as much time with them as possible.
- Grief is experienced in doses over years, not quickly and efficiently. As you encounter your pain, you will need the continued support of your friends and family for a long time to come. If you are not getting the support you need, ask for it. Usually people are more than willing to help, but they don't know what to do (or what not to do).

CARPE DIEM
Make a list of the things that would be helpful for others to take care of. Send an email or a text to your three closest friends letting them know what would help you the most right now.

10.

ALLOW FOR NUMBNESS

"God has mercifully ordered that the human brain works slowly. First the blow; hours afterwards, the bruise."
— Walter de la Mare

- Feelings of shock, numbness, and disbelief are nature's way of temporarily protecting us from the full reality of a sudden, traumatic loss. They help us survive our early grief.

- We often think, "I will wake up and this will not have happened." Early grief, especially, can feel like being in a dream.

- Your emotions need time to catch up with what your mind has been told.

- Even after you have moved beyond these initial feelings, don't be surprised if they re-emerge. Birthdays, holidays, and anniversaries often trigger these normal and necessary feelings.

- Traumatic (sudden and disturbing or violent) loss often results in more than what we consider "normal" shock. In fact, you may experience what is called "psychic numbing"—the deadening or shutting off of emotions. Your sense that "this isn't happening to me" may persist for weeks or months. Don't set rigid expectations for yourself and your ability to function "normally" in the world around you.

- Think of shock and numbness as a bandage that your psyche has placed over your wound. The bandage protects the wound until it has become less open and raw. Only after healing has begun is the bandage removed and the wound openly exposed to the world.

CARPE DIEM

If you're feeling numb, cancel any commitments that require concentration and decision-making. Allow yourself time to regroup.

11.

CONSIDER YOURSELF IN EMOTIONAL INTENSIVE CARE

"Rest is not idleness, and to lie sometimes on the grass under trees on a summer's day, listening to the murmur of the water, or watching the clouds float across the sky, is by no means a waste of time."
— John Lubbock

- Something catastrophic has happened in your life. Something assaulting to the very core of your being. Something excruciatingly painful.

- Your spirit has been deeply injured. Just as your body cannot be expected to recover immediately after a miscarriage, neither can your psyche.

- Imagine that you've suffered a severe physical injury and are in your hospital's intensive care unit. Your friends and family surround you with their presence and love. The medical staff attends to you constantly. Your body rests and recovers.

- This is the kind of emotional and spiritual care you need and deserve right now. The blow you have suffered is no less devastating than this imagined physical injury. Allow others to take care of you. Ask for their help. Give yourself as much resting time as possible. Take time off work. Let household chores slide. In the early days and weeks after your loss, don't expect—indeed, don't try—to carry on with your normal routine.

CARPE DIEM

Close your eyes and imagine yourself in "emotional intensive care." Where are you? What kind of care are you receiving? From whom? Arrange a weekend or a week of the emotional and spiritual intensive care you most need.

12.

KNOW THERE IS NO ORDER TO GRIEF

"Serenity is not freedom from the storm, but peace amid the storm."
— Unknown

- Grief is anything but orderly and predictable. You are not going to move through a series of stages toward some particular end point. If you can, consider your grief a meandering journey without a fixed destination.

- Though the needs of mourning are numbered 1 through 6 in the previous pages, it's important to understand that grief is not an ordered progression toward hope and healing. Don't fall into the trap of thinking your grief journey will be predictable or always forward-moving. Mourning is really a process that unfolds in its own unique way depending on how you choose to express yourself.

- Usually, grief hurts more before it begins to hurt less. Sometimes it will feel as if you are taking two steps forward and one step back.

- You will probably experience a multitude of different emotions in a wave-like fashion. You will also likely be working on more than one need of mourning at a time. This is normal.

- Be compassionate and patient with yourself as you experience your own unique grief journey.

CARPE DIEM

If you have read about or been told about the "stages" of grief, remember this is not how your grief will proceed. Don't allow yourself or others to tell you how, when, and what your grief should be like.

13.

KEEP A JOURNAL

"This pouring thoughts out on paper has relieved me.
I feel better and full of confidence and resolution."
— Diet Eman

- Journals are an ideal way for some mourners to express their thoughts and feelings—in other words, to mourn.

- Remember—your inner thoughts and feelings of grief need to be expressed outwardly (which includes writing) if you are to heal.

- Consider jotting down your thoughts and feelings about this miscarriage first thing when you wake up or each night before you go to sleep. Your journal entries can be as long or as short as you want.

- Don't worry about what you're writing or how well you're writing it. Just write whatever comes into your mind. To get started, set a timer for five or ten minutes and write as much as you can without stopping.

- After a sudden, unexpected loss, it can feel like you're stuck in your grief. Keeping a journal will allow you to look back at early entries months from now and see the progress you've made.

CARPE DIEM
Stop by your local bookstore and choose a blank book you like
the look and feel of. Visit a park on your way home,
find a quiet bench, and write your first entry.

14.

SHARE THE EXPERIENCE OF THE MISCARRIAGE ITSELF

"We are all the pieces of what we remember."
— Cassandra Clare

- With early miscarriage, it's common for families never to see a baby. Sometimes the baby didn't develop enough to look like a baby. Sometimes blood and tissue are released in a way or place that they're not seen by the parents. And sometimes parents feel traumatized by the blood or tissue that they *did* see.

- The invisible or, conversely, visibly traumatic nature of miscarriage can complicate your grief. You may struggle with whether or not there even *was* a baby. After all, how can you grieve for someone who never existed? Or you may struggle more with the violent, painful, or bloody reality.

- As we discussed in the Introduction, miscarriage and ectopic pregnancy take place during a liminal time. They lie betwixt and between "before life" and "life." Still, while you may never have seen a baby, you do know what it was like to be *expecting* a baby. Of this you can be certain. Now you must mourn the reality that you are no longer expecting and that your life will be different than you thought it would be.

CARPE DIEM

Talk to someone you trust about what you saw or did not see during or after your miscarriage. Acknowledging the reality of your loss is a vital part of your grief journey, yet you may feel uncertain about what you lost and how it happened. Sometimes just talking this through will help you begin to come to terms with the reality of your unique loss.

15.

FIND WAYS TO MAKE PEACE WITH THE DISPOSITION

"We never lose our loved ones. They accompany us; they don't disappear from our lives. We are merely in different rooms."

— Paulo Coelho

- Many couples struggle with what happened to the baby's body or to the lost tissue after the miscarriage. While stillborn babies (after 20 weeks' gestation) are treated as babies and funeral homes usually handle the bodies, hospitals typically treat miscarried babies and D&C tissue as medical waste, which is usually incinerated. Often the tissue is sent to pathology for examination beforehand.

- In hospitals in some states, like Massachusetts, parents are given the choice of what to do with miscarried remains. More and more hospitals and states are considering respectful disposition policies and laws. But in most states, the law still dictates that the above process be followed.

- Of course, many miscarriages occur at home, and parents must decide for themselves what to do with the blood and tissue. In the chaos and pain of the moment, it's common—and understandable—for the remains to be placed in the trash or toilet.

- Because of the liminal nature of miscarriage and also the wide range of miscarriage circumstances, there are no simple answers to the question of disposition. If you are among those who are struggling with what was or wasn't done after your miscarriage, talk about your concerns with your partner and others. Expressing your thoughts and feelings is the most important thing to do.

- It's not too late to have a simple burial or ceremony. Sometimes clothing and other mementos can be buried or cremated. One couple arranged with a cemetery for burial of a microscope slide of cells, which the hospital pathologist was able to provide.

CARPE DIEM

If you or your partner have questions or concerns about the disposition of the body or tissue, talk about it today. Invite someone who is creative and compassionate to join in the conversation. Maybe the three of you can come up with a way that feels right to honor the physical reality of this baby.

16.

BE COMPASSIONATE WITH YOUR PARTNER

"If you want others to be happy, practice compassion.
If you want to be happy, practice compassion."
— Dalai Lama

- The pain of this loss has likely rippled into the lives of many other people in your life. Some of them may be grieving this baby's loss as deeply as you are, especially your partner.

- Because your experiences with this loss may be so different from one another's, you may not recognize your partner's behaviors or emotions as grief. Be as compassionate and nonjudgmental as you can about your partner's reactions to your miscarriage.

- Grieving parents often are not able to support one another well in the grief journey. When we are grieving, our need to feel understood is high, and our ability to understand others is low. You and your partner may simply be too overcome with your own thoughts and feelings about your loss to be truly helpful to each other right now. This is normal, not a sign of relationship failure.

- Mothers often feel more affected by the loss. In fact, some research has shown that a mother's grief can be more disabling and longer lasting. Women also tend to be more outwardly emotional and slower to return to daily routines than men. It's important not to compare your grief, however, because your experiences with the baby were not the same.

- Fathers often feel the same depth of grief after the loss of a baby, though these feelings are sometimes not expressed because of expectations society has placed on men in grief. Men may appear more stoic, and they may want to return to work faster. That being said, it is also important to know that in some relationships these roles are reversed.

- If you are not in a committed relationship with a loving partner, you will need to look to others for daily support and compassion. You cannot do this alone. You deserve help.

CARPE DIEM
Take 10 minutes or more today to sit down with your partner.
Talk with one another without accusing or judging. Look at each other,
connect by holding each other's hands, and talk about any
unreconciled feelings you have about your miscarriage.

17.

BE LOVING TOWARD YOUR CHILDREN

"There is something you must always remember. You are braver than you believe, stronger than you seem, and smarter than you think."
—Winnie the Pooh

- If you have other children, they too are experiencing the pain of this loss in their own unique way. Grieving siblings are often "forgotten mourners." This means that parents, extended family, friends, and society tend to overlook that they have also experienced a significant loss.

- If the children knew about the expected baby, they will grieve. If they did not know, they will still sense your grief, creating a kind of a secondary grief.

- Children may not express grief directly and, instead, indirectly demonstrate to others that they are struggling. They may show some regressive behaviors, like wanting to sleep with mom and dad, clinging to parents more often, or asking to be taken care of in ways they were when they were younger. They may also display sadness or anxiety through behaviors such as irritability, anger, distractibility, decreased motivation at school, and disorganization. If supportive grown-ups can help grieving siblings find more direct and healthy ways of coping with their grief, these behaviors will lessen.

- What grieving siblings need most is for adults to be open and honest with them about the miscarriage. They need to know that it is okay to talk about the baby and what happened. They need their questions answered and their unique thoughts and feelings acknowledged.

- Pay attention to how much your grief consumes your household day in and day out. Your children have daily needs—school, activities, nutrition, hygiene, social events. Your home should still be a sanctuary for your children.

CARPE DIEM

Gather together as a family in a comfortable room in the house.
Go around and have each person share how he or she is feeling since
the miscarriage. You may uncover some memories, fears, or questions
that you didn't know were present in the house.

18.

IF YOU'VE HAD INFERTILITY PROBLEMS, KNOW THAT THIS WILL COMPLICATE YOUR GRIEF

"When it's dark enough, you can see the stars."
— Ralph Waldo Emerson

- A miscarriage following infertility diagnostics and treatment can be especially painful. A hoped-for pregnancy was finally achieved…only to be taken away. Understandably, this can create profound feelings of anger, heartache, and despair.

- Keep in mind the rule of thumb we discussed in the Introduction: The more you wanted this baby, the more invested you were in your hopes and dreams for a child, the more painful and complicated your grief journey will likely be. Couples who dedicate the commitment, time, and expense required for fertility diagnostics and treatment are deeply invested in their pregnancies, so their loss can seem a particularly cruel and unfair outcome.

- Of course, infertility itself is a form of loss, so it, too, produces grief and requires mourning.

- "Complicated grief" simply means that you may need extra help working through and expressing your thoughts and feelings. Consider attending a support group for infertile couples and/or seeing a compassionate counselor who has experience with miscarriage grief.

CARPE DIEM
Look into infertility support groups or grief counseling today.

19.

IF YOU'VE HAD MORE THAN ONE MISCARRIAGE, SEEK EXTRA SUPPORT

"How much tragedy has to happen before I split wide open?"
— Alisa Mullen

- Couples who experience more than one miscarriage are faced with grief upon grief.

- While a second miscarriage will usually trigger more medical testing—which may reveal a cause that can be corrected for the next pregnancy—this does not erase existing losses. And sometimes a cause can't be identified, creating the prospect of more loss in the future.

- People who suffer multiple losses of any kind during the same time frame or back-to-back are said to be experiencing "grief overload." In other words, they have been burdened with a degree of loss that would understandably exceed anyone's capacity to cope.

- If you've had more than one miscarriage and find yourself struggling, I encourage you to seek out a compassionate, experienced grief counselor who can support and encourage you as you mourn. You deserve and may well need extra help in the weeks and months to come.

CARPE DIEM
If you don't already have a trusted grief counselor,
ask your friends and family members for a referral today.

20.

IF YOU OR YOUR PARTNER WERE AMBIVALENT ABOUT THE PREGNANCY, KNOW THAT THIS CAN COMPLICATE YOUR GRIEF

"I slide to my knees and say, 'Please let this be over.'
Then I'm not ready for it to be over."
— Andre Agassi

- In the Introduction to this book, I said that the more you wanted this baby, the more invested you were in your hopes and dreams for a child, the more painful and complicated your grief journey will likely be. This is true. But it's also true that ambivalence, which means having mixed or contradictory feelings about something, can create painful, complicated grief.

- If you or your partner weren't sure you wanted this child, your grief journey will be affected by this ambivalence. The miscarriage might have felt partly like a loss and partly like a relief. Or the miscarriage may seem like punishment for not wanting the baby enough, which can in turn result in feelings of guilt and regret. And between partners, mismatched degrees of wanting a pregnancy that ended in miscarriage can fuel blame and anger.

- Know that ambivalence is normal in any relationship. We love the people in our lives, but we also can be annoyed with, angry at, and tired of them, right? Human emotion is always complex and multidimensional. Your ambivalence about the pregnancy is not unusual or wrong. Feelings are not right or wrong—they just *are*.

- Complicated grief means that you might need extra support in the weeks and months to come. A compassionate, skilled grief counselor could help you work through any feelings of guilt, regret, blame, anger, and ambivalence.

CARPE DIEM
If you or your partner were ambivalent about this pregnancy, talk to someone about your mixed feelings today.

21.

CRY

"Tears have a wisdom all their own. They come when a person has relaxed enough to let go and to work through his sorrow. They are the natural bleeding of an emotional wound, carrying the poison out of the system. Here lies the road to recovery."

— F. Alexander Magoun

- It is not only OK to cry, it's healing. Cry alone, cry in the presence of friends, cry in the presence of strangers. Allow yourself to cry when your tears well up, wanting to be released. You may find yourself crying at unexpected times and places. Over time you will come to predict what will trigger your tears.

- Tears are your body's way of naturally cleansing and healing itself. After a loss, we naturally feel hurt, helpless, and vulnerable. Your tears are an expression of these feelings. Tears communicate to those around you (and to yourself) that you are carrying pain that needs release. Through your tears your grief moves from the inside out.

- If you are not crying a lot, that's OK too. Not everyone is a crier. You may still be in shock about your miscarriage. Or you may be finding other ways to move your grief from the inside to the outside. If you are unsure of how others will respond to your tears or if you feel tears are a sign of weakness, this may also keep you from releasing them. Remind yourself that tears are a result of the privilege of giving and receiving love.

- You may find that others are uncomfortable with your tears. They may not know what to say when you cry. They may try to soothe you by saying, "Don't cry" or "Tears won't help." Let your friends and family know that you need to cry right now and that they can help you most by allowing you to cry as often, as loudly, and as embarrassingly as you need to.

CARPE DIEM
Find a place where you know you can allow yourself to cry—in your car, in the shower, into your pillow, in the arms of someone you love.
Take time today to release some of your tears.
Cry as long and as hard as your body needs.

22.

DESIGNATE A TIME TO MOURN EACH DAY

"Many people are alive but don't touch the miracle of being alive."
— Thich Nhat Hanh

- Mourning is exhausting work. It is often something that we try hard to prevent, avoid, or deny.

- In an effort to move toward your grief rather than away from it, consider making mourning part of your daily routine. When it hurts, you know mourning is working. It is helping you integrate and transform your grief. Just like the other ways you take care of yourself— taking a shower, eating a healthy meal, going for a walk—mourning is a way of taking care of your grieving self.

- Set aside a quiet time each day, even if it is only five minutes. Use this time to consciously focus on your thoughts and feelings about your miscarriage.

- The first ten minutes after you wake up might be a good time to do this, like a release of emotion prior to entering the day. This also might be a good time to journal about what surfaces.

- Creating a dedicated mourning time may allow you to concentrate on truly living rather than merely existing as you move through the rest of your day.

CARPE DIEM

Conscious mourning sounds absurd, I know. Purposefully invite pain into my day? Yet it will come without warning anyway, because it demands to be seen and heard. Giving it a dedicated time and space each day may help you meet all your other obligations even as you do the necessary work of mourning.

23.

UNDERSTAND WHEN OTHERS SAY, "I'M SORRY"

"Apology is a lovely perfume; it can transform the clumsiest moment into a gracious gift."

— Margaret Lee Runbeck

- Many grieving parents have told me that they find it unhelpful when others say, "I'm sorry." Somehow these words lose their meaning when they are said too often.

- You may wonder what they are sorry for. After all, they were not responsible for this tragedy. You may think, "I don't need you to be sorry. I need you to wrap your arms around me (or do my grocery shopping or sit and really talk with me) so that I know I am not alone right now."

- If you are wondering how you are supposed to respond to the common utterance "I'm sorry," perhaps it would help if you knew what the person actually means:

  "I'm sorry that you are going through this pain and that there is nothing I can do to take it away."

- This is something many people you encounter will feel for you. When others hear your story or see you express your pain, they will be inclined to want to fix it or fast-forward you through it. Not only is pain hard to feel, it's hard to watch.

- Before your miscarriage, perhaps you yourself offered this compassionate response to another human being mired in grief—a friend, a parent, your partner, or one of your children. Indeed, there is nothing anyone can say or do to take away the pain because the pain is a necessary part of loss.

CARPE DIEM

Think about what you will say to the next person who tells you she is sorry. Maybe you could respond by sharing more of your experience, which will help you mourn and also educate her about miscarriage loss.

24.

TAKE TIME OFF WORK

"People, even more than things, have to be restored, renewed, revived, reclaimed, and redeemed; never throw out anyone."
— Sam Levenson

- Especially in the early days after a miscarriage, take some time off work if at all possible. In addition to the need for your body to recover, your spirit needs time to adjust to the new reality and to mourn. Your grief takes priority right now.

- We've said that our culture can be unaware of or insensitive to the grief of couples who've miscarried. This extends to the workplace, of course.

- Some companies have flexible bereavement leave policies that allow people to take paid leave after a miscarriage. Women who work for a larger company are entitled to unpaid leave under the Family and Medical Leave Act.

- When you return to work, try to be open with your coworkers about your miscarriage experience. Telling your story is important to your mourning, as is reaching out for and accepting the help of others. If they don't know what's happened and how it's affected you, they won't be able to help.

- Consider talking to your boss and a human resources staff member about your miscarriage too. You will be doing your part to make your workplace more sensitive and compassionate to all types of loss.

CARPE DIEM

If you're concerned about work for any reason in the weeks after your miscarriage—because of financial challenges, not having enough energy to meet demands, needing to stay home instead of travel, etc.—talk to your supervisor about it. Open, proactive communication is almost always the best antidote to worry.

25.

IF YOU FEEL GUILTY, FIND WAYS TO EXPRESS IT

"Guilt isn't always a rational thing. Guilt is a weight that will crush you whether you deserve it or not."

— Maureen Johnson

- If you are feeling doubt or guilt about something related to your loss of this baby, it's important to pay attention to it. It can take time to work through these feelings. And this is important work, because exploring these feelings now will help ensure they don't weigh you down later.

- After a miscarriage, some parents feel guilty that they didn't do everything perfectly during the pregnancy. Some mothers feel they weren't protective or nurturing enough to their bodies. Some experience guilt that they didn't know something was wrong. Do you run things over and over in your mind to try to identify what could have happened?

- Yet if you are reading this book, I am certain that you loved this baby. You cared for this baby. You are not perfect, but no one is. Do you believe you were responsible for the baby's conception? Or was some greater power responsible for that miracle? Is it possible that the miscarriage was equally in the hands of a greater power?

- Talk openly with your partner, a supportive friend, or a counselor about any feelings of doubt and guilt. Feeding these feelings by thinking about them over and over again and continuing to punish yourself is not going to help you, your partner, or, if you have them, other children. Give these feelings of doubt and guilt a voice. Expressing them may diminish the power they have over you right now.

- Rationally or irrationally, some parents blame their partners for some aspect of the miscarriage. If feelings of blame reside in you, talk compassionately to your partner, perhaps with the help of a counselor. Remember that his or her heart is also broken.

CARPE DIEM
If you have feelings of doubt, regret, or guilt about your miscarriage, talk to someone about them today.

26.

IF YOU FEEL ANGRY, FIND WAYS TO EXPRESS IT

"Holding on to anger is like grasping a hot coal with the intent of throwing it at someone else; you are the one who gets burned."

— Buddha

- Anger is a normal and necessary emotion after loss. It's our way of protesting a reality we don't like. It's an emotional defense against the fear that surfaces when loss enters our lives. Anger gives us a sense of control when we experience something that we were unable to control. It also helps mask the more passive yet painful feelings of sadness and despair.

- Logically or illogically, you may feel angry at others around you, sometimes for no reason other than that your baby died and their baby did not. You may be angry at other mothers who are giving birth at the hospital, at pregnant women you see, at your partner for his response to your miscarriage, at your doctor for his non-emotional response to your loss or for not listening to your concerns during pregnancy, or at your mother or best friend because they aren't being as supportive as you'd like.

- Like all of your feelings, anger is not wrong. It simply is. What you do with your anger can be wrong, however. If you are angry and isolate yourself in anger, you may slide into chronic depression. Express anger in healthy ways. Never harm yourself or someone else in an attempt to squelch your rage. This will only hurt you in the end.

CARPE DIEM

Today, if you feel angry, vent your anger through physical activity. Run instead of walk. Go for a hike. Throw rocks across a lake or in a field. Punch a boxing bag. Or if your body isn't ready for strenuous activity yet, write an angry journal entry or a letter that you don't send.

27.

IF YOU FEEL ENVIOUS, FIND WAYS TO EXPRESS IT

"Envy is the art of counting the other fellow's blessings instead of your own."
— Harold Coffin

- In the aftermath of pregnancy loss, it's common to feel envious of other women who are pregnant or have healthy babies. "Why them and not me?" you might understandably wonder. "It's not fair!" You're right. It's not fair.

- Women who are pregnant or who've just delivered babies are cared for by the same doctors and nurses who care for women who've miscarried. You will be on the same hospital floor or in the same waiting rooms. This may seem cruel to you now.

- Try to remember that envy, like all other emotions, is not right or wrong. It just is. Like its close cousin, anger, envy is what I call a protest emotion—an emotion that protests a reality you don't want to be true. Underneath protest emotions are fear and sadness.

- The next time you feel pregnancy or baby envy, try expressing it. Tell your partner or a close friend. Write about it in your journal. Share in an online forum.

- Or, reach out—kindly—to the woman or family you feel envious of. Say congratulations. If the circumstances are right, tell her about your loss. She just might have stories of her own to share. Connecting and communicating are healing actions.

CARPE DIEM
Make an action plan for what you will do the next time you feel envious. How can you use the feeling as a positive catalyst for healing?

28.

IF YOU FEEL AFRAID, FIND WAYS TO EXPRESS IT

"No one ever told me that grief felt so much like fear."
— C.S. Lewis

- Couples who've experienced miscarriage often feel afraid. Mothers fear they might have done something to cause the miscarriage. Partners fear they didn't do enough to help the pregnant mother. They both fear the prospect of the difficult weeks and months ahead without this pregnancy and baby. Understandably, it's also common for them to fear what could happen with another pregnancy.

- Fear and sadness are probably the two most challenging emotions to befriend. Yet both arise because they need to be experienced and worked through.

- Fear tends to soften the more it's expressed. Talk about your fears with your partner and others who are close to you. Share your fears in the compassionate context of a support group. Give voice to your fears and watch them diminish.

- Practicing living in the moment is another effective way to counteract fear. For the most part, fear inhabits the imagined future. Is your present moment scary? Are you or is someone you care about in danger right this minute? If not, work on redirecting your fearful mind to observing the now. Notice and appreciate what is around you, what you can actually see. Pay attention to the sounds, tastes, textures, and smells. When your mind strays again, bring it back by focusing on your breath.

CARPE DIEM
What is your biggest fear since your miscarriage?
Talk to someone about it today.

29.

IF YOU FEEL DISAPPOINTED, FIND WAYS TO EXPRESS IT

"It was one of those times you feel a sense of loss, even though you didn't have something in the first place. I guess that's what disappointment is— a sense of loss for something you never had."

— Deb Caletti

- Couples who've suffered a miscarriage often use the word "disappointed" to describe their sadness. The term captures the sense of hope and joy they had for the pregnancy, followed by a feeling of emptiness and loss after the joy is taken away.

- Disappointment is what you're left with whenever your expectations are not met. It's the down after the up. The higher the up, the deeper the down.

- Your grief probably includes deep disappointment, among many other emotions. Disappointment hurts. Disappointment can be shattering.

- It's normal, natural, and necessary for you to feel disappointed after this miscarriage. Now take the next step and express it.

CARPE DIEM

If you feel disappointment over the miscarriage, talk to your partner about it. Describe the hopes and dreams you had for this baby in detail. This will help both you and your partner understand what you feel you have lost for the future.

30.

JUST BE

"The Western mind is obsessed by doing more and more, restless and constantly on the run, just cannot sit still into being the grace that descends...just by being...still, being leads to being."
— Swami Rajneesh

- Sometimes what we need most is just to "be." In our goal-oriented society, many of us have lost the knack for slowing down and living more simply.

- Here is a real challenge for you: Drop all of your plans and obligations for today and do nothing.

- Another way to just "be" is to practice some form of meditation. Meditation can help center you, slow down your racing thoughts, and relax your physical body. Meditation is simply quiet, relaxed contemplation. You need not follow any particular rules or techniques, although learning proper ways of breathing can help you gain a deeper state of stillness. Simply find a place where you can focus on whatever flows in and out of your mind. When you are distracted by noises, people, or tasks, just bring your mind back to your breath. This may take some practice!

- Find someplace quiet, be still, close your eyes, and focus on breathing in and out. Listen to your breath. Notice your muscles relaxing as you exhale tension. Perhaps you will find such stillness that you will be able to hear your own heartbeat. If in this moment your mind wanders to thoughts of your miscarriage, allow yourself to have the thought and then move your attention back to your breath.

CARPE DIEM

Sit down and hold something soft in your hands (such as a teddy bear or blanket). Focus on just feeling the object and take 10 deep breaths. Breathe in and fill your belly with your inhale rather than filling your chest. Then, slightly slower than when you breathed in, let the air out of your belly.

31.

OPEN YOUR HEART

"I've learned that whenever I decide something with an open heart,
I usually make the right decision."

— Maya Angelou

- When we experience loss, our first response is almost always to close ourselves off, to protect our heart and soul from experiencing more pain. We sometimes will even find ourselves guarded or closed off from the people we love the most—our partner, our surviving children, our parents.

- Opening your heart can be difficult when you have experienced such a painful loss. But it is not impossible. Perhaps through meditation you can visualize your open heart, or through yoga you can embody your open heart through poses that open your chest. If you do not practice meditation or yoga, try sitting and using your imagination to make space in your heart, enough space to let at least one person in for right now. You can continue to work on expanding this, but opening to even one person right now is a good start.

- Open hearts allow love to flow in as well as out.

CARPE DIEM

Try reflecting on this thought: "As I allow myself to mourn,
I create an opening in my heart. Releasing the tensions of grief,
surrendering to the struggle, means freeing myself to go forward
and allowing myself to love and be loved."

32.

REMEMBER: ONE DAY AT A TIME

---

*"Enjoy the little things, for one day you may look back and
realize they were the big things."*
— Robert Brault

- Powerful emotions stemming from grief may lead you to believe you
  will never be happy again, or at least not as happy as you were. It's
  important to acknowledge those emotions and this belief that feels so
  true to you right now.

- It's equally important to remind yourself that despite how you feel at
  this moment, you will continue to grow and live one breath at a time.

- If you focus on being able to take one breath in and one breath out
  at a time, and then one hour at a time, and then one day at a time,
  with loving support and time you will again experience joy. The joy
  you feel may not be the same; you are right about that. Why? Because
  experiencing loss changes you. You are not the same person you were
  before your miscarriage, and part of your grief journey entails getting
  reacquainted with your new self.

- At the beginning of each day, take note that it is a new day and that
  new opportunities await you.

CARPE DIEM

It is important to reestablish structure in your days when you feel ready.
Make a checklist of what you need to do and then prioritize what needs
to be done. Check off what you complete. Try immersing yourself and be
present in each activity, even if it's only for a few minutes. Use your breath
to anchor you into the present moment throughout the day.

33.

UNDERSTAND WHAT IT MEANS TO BE "TRAUMATIZED"

"Sometimes a breakdown can be the beginning of a kind of breakthrough, a way of living in advance through a trauma that prepares you for a future of radical transformation."

— Cherrie Moraga

- A miscarriage is usually sudden and unexpected, and for many parents, the experience can be traumatic. If your miscarriage itself was painful, bloody, or horrific in any way, you probably suffered some degree of trauma.

- Grief after a traumatic loss is often different than grief after an anticipated or "peaceful" loss. Significant loss always causes painful feelings, but in the case of sudden, violent loss, your mind has an especially difficult time coming to terms with the circumstances of the loss itself.

- In this sense, the word "trauma" refers to intense feelings of shock, fear, anxiety, and helplessness surrounding the event of the miscarriage. Trauma is caused by events of such intensity and physical violence that they would overwhelm any human being's capacity to cope.

- Certainly it can be said that death is always traumatic. Even the natural death of an elderly parent can feel traumatic to her children. But sudden, violent loss results in a kind of psychic injury and typically involves frightening and often intrusive thoughts about the distressful hours of the loss event. Finding ways to process your trauma will be an important part of your grief journey.

CARPE DIEM

How is the traumatic nature of your miscarriage shaping your grief right now? If you feel traumatized by the event of the miscarriage, talk to someone you trust about this today.

34.

MAKE AN INVENTORY OF SURVIVAL STRATEGIES

"We each survive in our own way."

— Sarah J. Maas

- Survival is one step followed by the next... followed by the next. What has helped you cope with stress and loss in the past? These strategies will probably help you now too.

- Each of us has coping skills that we have used in times of distress. Sometimes our coping strategies are effective and healthy; other times we fall back on them simply because they are what is familiar to us. They have worked "well enough" that we continue to return to them when we are struggling.

- Make a list of the most difficult times in your life and the ways in which you helped yourself live through them. Did you spend time with family? Write? Turn to your faith? Help take care of someone else? Which activities calm you? Getting a massage, talking a walk, going for a swim, talking to your sister on the phone, walking the dog, reading a book, meditating? These are the survival techniques that you want to try to use today and every day.

- Make note of any of these that are unhealthy ways of managing your suffering, such as substance abuse, gambling, or overeating, for example. We want to be sure these are not the coping skills you turn to during this difficult time. For most of us, it takes the routine use of a new coping skill over several weeks to replace any old habits or strategies that are detrimental.

CARPE DIEM

Make a list of what you need to get through the next week. This could include more time alone, more time with others, daily tasks that are hanging over your head, or something you really want to do but don't have the capacity to plan right now. Looking ahead a week at a time may seem less overwhelming than thinking about months or the next year. Ask your friends and family to help if your list contains items that you know you will not be able to accomplish on your own.

35.

RELINQUISH CONTROL

"When I let go of what I am, I become what I might be.
When I let go of what I have, I receive what I need."
— Tao Te Ching

- Modern medical technology is wonderful, but it can give us a false sense of control over early pregnancy. We can now test for ovulation, time sex to optimize the chance of fertilization, take a home pregnancy test before our period is even due, and see the baby and a heartbeat on ultrasound at just a few weeks' gestation. We can have in vitro. We can have tests done on the baby in utero to check for all kinds of diseases and abnormalities. Surgery can even be done on the baby in utero for certain problems.

- But even though technology makes our pregnancy experiences different and often safer than those of our grandmothers (perhaps creating different understandings of and sensitivities to early pregnancy loss among generations), we still are not in total control of life and death.

- Part of your grief journey will involve surrendering yourself to your new reality as well as to your inability to control what might happen with a subsequent pregnancy. Of course, we don't like not having control because it makes us feel helpless.

- You can't let go of your grief or loss because it is now part of you. But you can learn to let go of the illusion of control.

CARPE DIEM
Talk to someone about any feelings of helplessness or lack of control you have felt because of your miscarriage.

36.

BE PATIENT

"When we lose those we love, we must understand that it takes time to learn to feel again. For nothing can touch the heart that is frozen with grief."
— Unknown

- I'm sure you've realized by now that healing in grief does not happen quickly. Remember, grief is not something we truly ever "get over." You will spend a lifetime continuing to integrate this loss into your being and someday, instead of carrying the heavy, compressing, painful grief you may feel right now, you will carry your integrated grief. When grief is integrated, your loss will still be a part of you, but it will not weigh heavy or slow you down.

- In our hurried North American culture, patience can be especially hard to find. It's a behavior that is becoming less and less commonplace, as we are all rushing around and trying to do everything at once. With technology expanding at such a fast rate, just about everything is at our fingertips. Over the past couple decades, we have all been conditioned to believe that if we want something, we should be able to get it instantly.

- Yet patience, not urgency, is vital in grief. Your grief will not heed anyone's timetable—including your own. Be patient with your body, mind, and spirit. Be patient with those around you if they are not where you want them to be in their own grief. Just as you are, they are doing the best they can.

CARPE DIEM

When you are feeling impatient, silently repeat this phrase: "My grief is on its own course. It will take its time, and if I fight it, it will take more time."

37.

LET GO OF DESTRUCTIVE MISCONCEPTIONS ABOUT GRIEF AND MOURNING

"People suffer because they are caught in their views. As soon as we release those views, we are free and we don't suffer anymore."
— Thich Nhat Hanh

- Along the way it's natural for all of us to internalize many of our culture's harmful misconceptions about grief and mourning. You probably recognize the following:

  Don't cry. Tears are a sign of weakness.

  People need to get over their grief and just put it behind them.

  Death is a taboo topic. It's something we don't talk about.

  When other people are counting on you, you need to "hurry up and deal with it" and get things back to "normal."

- If you buy into these misconceptions, they will often cause you to put pressure on yourself to heal. They will also bring up new emotions for you to deal with, including guilt or shame about your true thoughts and feelings related to the death of your baby.

- Remind yourself that these misconceptions are not rules to grieve by. In fact, they will take you off course and delay your grief most of the time. Your grief is what it is, and it's unique, not exactly like anyone else's, even the grief of others who have experienced miscarriage. It's normal and necessary.

CARPE DIEM

Which grief misconception has been most harmful to your grief journey?
Consider the ways in which you can help teach others about
these destructive misconceptions.

38.

WEAR A SYMBOL OF MOURNING

"He that conceals his grief finds no remedy for it."
— Turkish proverb

- In centuries past, mourners identified themselves in some way to communicate that they were torn apart and in the process of grieving after the death of someone loved. Wearing jewelry or wreaths made out of locks of hair that belonged to the person who died were common practices. Black clothing, or mourning clothes, were required to be worn for a period of one year. Sometimes mourners wore black armbands.

- These symbols of mourning accorded a special status to mourners, saying, in effect, "Someone I love has died. Please offer me your respect and condolences." Today we no longer identify mourners in these ways, creating the harmful illusion that "everything is back to normal"—even thought it's not and never will be.

- As we've said, miscarriage in particular is socially invisible. The pregnancy may never have been apparent to others, creating a false sense of normalcy after the miscarriage.

- How can you let others know you're still in mourning and continue to need their support? The best way is to tell them. Talk about your miscarriage and its continuing impact on your life. Let your friends and family know you still need reassurance, love, and help.

CARPE DIEM
Make a symbol of your loss part of your everyday dress. Wear a certain piece of jewelry, such as a necklace or bracelet. Some people choose jewelry designs that incorporate angel wings or hearts. Others wear black bracelets or armbands. Our Center for Loss has an "Under Reconstruction" pin you might be interested in, available at www.centerforloss.com.

39.

KNOW THERE ARE NO BAD DAYS, ONLY "NECESSARY" DAYS

"It is no use saying, 'We are doing our best.'
You have got to succeed in doing what is necessary."
— Winston Churchill

- Many parents talk about having "bad" days more often than not after a miscarriage. What they mean is that they have spent a majority of the day crying, feeling extremely sad, or unable to really engage in anything productive. These are days that you likely dread and that make you feel as if you are not making progress toward integrating this loss.

- Yet these "bad" days are actually days when your body and mind have insisted that you mourn. What would happen if you were able to perceive them as "necessary" instead of bad?

- It may be difficult to give yourself permission to just embrace these days. Because they surface without warning, embracing them may seem impossible. If you could plan for them, that would make it easier. Over time your grief will not shanghai you like this. It will not take over your life so thoroughly, from hour to hour, and day to day.

- If the tears and sorrow still enter your days and engulf you for hours, give yourself permission to fully relinquish your day to your grief. Think of it as a mental health day and give yourself the day to sit with and befriend your grief. It may not be the way you would like to spend a day off of work, but befriending your grief and giving it attention is the only way it will stop demanding to be heard.

- So often our grief lingers because we are fighting it every step of the way. We are telling ourselves what we "should not" do—we should not still be crying or we should not still be so debilitated—rather than allowing ourselves to cry deeply, without pause.

CARPE DIEM
What does surrendering fully to your grief mean to you?
Describe to your partner or a companion in grief what the moment that you fully surrender to a wave of grief is like.

40.

REACH OUT TO OTHERS WHO TRULY UNDERSTAND YOUR PAIN

"It is not in the going down that we demonstrate resilience,
it is in the getting up again."
— Ingrid Poulson

- If at times you feel alone, I want to remind you that you never are. While it's impossible to know exactly how many women experience a miscarriage each year (as we discussed in the Introduction), we can say for certain that many millions of families the world over have suffered the miscarriage of a child they very much yearned for. That means there are countless other grieving parents out there who know and feel the pain enveloping your heart.

- These families understand that miscarriage can be a uniquely painful experience. While their experiences and their grief will not match yours exactly, they "get it."

- Reaching out, listening to what has helped another parent survive, embracing their empathy, welcoming their understanding of this unique loss, and hearing their messages of hope will make your journey more tolerable.

CARPE DIEM
When you are ready, look up area support groups or
Google online resources focused on helping parents after a miscarriage.
Find a place where others openly share their stories and can truly
empathize with your loss. Participate.

41.

BELIEVE IN YOUR CAPACITY TO HEAL

"When you are sorrowful, look again in your heart, and you shall see that in truth you are weeping for that which has been your delight."

— Kahlil Gibran

- I want you to know that you will find your way to the other side of this pain and grief you are experiencing right now. You will survive this loss, and the pain will not always be so present in your heart.

- Yes, the pain may be overwhelming at times, especially in the early days and weeks, but with the love and support of others, your grief will soften. Though you may not be able to even imagine it, you will again feel other emotions beyond grief—emotions like excitement, wonder, and joy. There will come a day when your miscarriage is not something you think about every day.

- Some parents who have lost a baby through miscarriage (or multiple pregnancies through repeat miscarriage) also struggle with feeling they don't *want* to survive. Surviving may feel too painful at times. While this feeling is normal and will pass, it is important that you talk with someone when you are feeling this level of hopelessness and despair.

- The only way to the other side is through—through the hopelessness, through the pain, through the wilderness of grief. One day in the not-too-distant future, you will feel that there is a purpose in your life and that life is worth living again.

- As you mourn over time and integrate painful thoughts, feelings, and memories, you may find yourself not simply surviving, but truly thriving. You may come to live with peace, joy, presence, and love in your everyday life. The remainder of your life can be full and satisfying if you choose to experience life fully rather than merely exist.

CARPE DIEM

If you are feeling that your grief feels unsurvivable, find a way to gain power over it. Draw a picture of it. Find a song that seems to articulate your grief experience more than your own words can. Give your grief a name, a face, or a voice. Expressing your grief in this way may diminish some of the power it has over you today.

42.

EMPOWER YOURSELF WITH INFORMATION

Always
Seek
Knowledge.
— Unknown

- Most parents who miscarry want to know why it happened. This is a normal and necessary question to ask.

- In the Introduction we reviewed the statistics about miscarriage. It is extremely common, especially in the first few weeks after conception. While the causes of miscarriage are not thoroughly understood, doctors do believe that most first-trimester miscarriages are caused by chromosomal abnormalities in the baby. These imperfections usually aren't caused by anything the mother or father did or genetics they carry. Most of the time they occur by random chance.

- Sometimes, though, doctors are able to pinpoint the cause of a miscarriage or of repeat miscarriage. Infections, hormonal problems, abnormalities of the uterus or cervix, underlying illness in the mother (such as autoimmune or kidney disease), and lifestyle choices such as smoking, drinking, and drug use can all result in miscarriage. Miscarriage rates also increase as women get older.

- In the chaotic, traumatic days surrounding your miscarriage, it's understandable if you weren't able to have a thorough conversation with your doctor about why the miscarriage may have happened. But now that some time has passed, you may be ready for more information.

- Blood and genetic tests as well as other diagnostic procedures are often helpful, especially after two miscarriages.

CARPE DIEM
Schedule a special appointment with your obstetric healthcare provider to talk about your miscarriage. Learning what you can about why it happened (even if the answer is that it was likely a chance occurrence) may help set your mind and heart at ease.

43.

MOVE TOWARD YOUR GRIEF, NOT AWAY FROM IT

"March on. Do not tarry. To go forward is to move toward perfection. March on, and fear not the thorns, or the sharp stones on life's path."
— Kahlil Gibran

- Our culture teaches us that emotional pain is to be avoided, not embraced. Others will advocate that it's better not to be in pain and encourage you to move away from your pain. Yet it is only in moving toward our grief that we can be healed.

- Remember, the only way to get to the other side is through.

- Be suspicious if you find yourself thinking that you or others are "doing well" since your miscarriage. Sometimes doing well means you are not allowing yourself to feel your grief and you are avoiding, denying, or minimizing the normal and necessary pain that follows significant loss.

- On the other hand, maybe you are doing well in moving toward your grief, and if so, I hope you will celebrate your progress!

- Of course, even if you are appropriately embracing your grief, it is also necessary to dose yourself with your painful thoughts and feelings. Sometimes you will need to distract yourself from the pain. But, in general, you should feel that you are leaning in to your grief.

CARPE DIEM
Take note of all of the people in your life who love you and were also excited about your pregnancy. Pick one or two of them to contact today, and talk about how you are feeling today about your miscarriage. Allow them to share their thoughts and feelings too.

44.

GIVE ATTENTION TO YOUR RELATIONSHIP

"Remember that a successful marriage depends on two things:
1) finding the right person and 2) being the right person."
— Author Unknown

- It's been said that divorce is more likely after parents lose a child. In my experience, however, this is no more true for you than it is for a couple who has not encountered a loss like yours.

- Grief is primarily a journey that transforms the self. You and your partner will not grieve in the same way, and while you will take the grief journey together, you will take different paths and trails. However, you can be there for each other as you each walk your own path and witness one another's grief. Talk about your experience, and listen to your partner's experience without trying to change it. Accept that you will have very different views of this pregnancy, of grief, of emotion, and of death.

- When a couple works on their relationship, this means they communicate about all that goes on in life. Marriages and committed relationships need attention every day. This miscarriage is just one part of your life together. Right now it may be the most painful part. Working on your relationship means talking openly about how this loss is influencing your daily life and how it is changing you. It also means spending time together, both in work and in play. It means figuring out the challenges, including financial stressors or differences in intimacy needs right now. It means sharing dreams and joys as well as failures and sorrows that are happening around you while you are both grieving this loss.

- People may say to you, "At least you have each other." This may not feel like a blessing in moments when you both are so overcome with grief. But in other moments it is wonderful to have a person you can count on, who is present to you and cares about how you feel.

CARPE DIEM

Look into a couples retreat or talk to your partner about meeting with someone who can help you open up about all of the ways this loss is affecting your relationship.

45.

EXPECT TO HAVE WHIRLWIND EMOTIONS

"Your intellect may be confused, but your emotions will never lie to you."
— Robert Ebert

- Your loss will probably not leave you feeling only sadness. Most people experience many other emotions in the wake of miscarriage, as well, such as numbness, anger, guilt, fear, worry, regret, confusion, and, for some parents, relief (in situations where the baby was not going to have a good quality of life even if she had survived, for example, or in cases in which parents were ambivalent about the pregnancy).

- Sometimes these feelings follow each other within a short period of time. Sometimes they may whirl together simultaneously, leaving you uncertain about what you are feeling. Think of these moments as a chord (many notes all at once) rather than a string of single notes one after another.

- As strange as some of your emotional moments may seem to you, I can assure you they are normal and healthy. At times, you may even feel like you are literally going crazy. Rest assured: it is the grief, and not you, that is crazy.

- Embracing the whirlwind as well as the single emotions is a difficult but necessary part of the journey. You may spend most of your day trying to avoid, prevent, or ignore the painful emotions from surfacing by keeping busy or distracting yourself. Every day, find a brief period of time that you can allow yourself to just feel whatever comes up. Without judging the feelings or yourself as good or bad, right or wrong, just feel. It may also help to put words to your grief when you make space and invite it to surface. Talk to a good listener or journal your feelings.

CARPE DIEM

Have your grief feelings surprised you? Which ones have been the most unexpected for you? Tell your partner or a friend about the surprising feelings and allow him to bear witness to your truth.

46.

TALK ABOUT GRIEF AND MOURNING

"Grief shared is grief diminished."
— Rabbi Earl Grollman

- To love and feel attached to another living being is to one day mourn. Because with every beginning there will be an ending. In every life there is also death. You have learned this most poignant of life's lessons.

- Maybe you could teach what you are learning about life, love, and loss to others. Tell your friends and family about the six needs of mourning. Share with them how important it is that mourners have others who companion them in grief rather than "treating" them as if they have an illness that needs to be cured.

- "Healing" your loss and "curing" your loss are two different concepts. Healing is an active emotional and spiritual process in which you seek to be whole again. Curing is a medical term that implies that someone or something outside of you rids you of your grief. Your grief cannot be cured; it will always live inside of you.

- Share your wisdom in the safety of a grief support group that focuses on supporting parents who have experienced pregnancy loss. Encourage the group to try to distinguish their grief from their process of mourning. Teach them what you know about this distinction.

- Remember that each person's grief journey is unique. Your grief journey will be influenced by many factors, including the circumstances of your miscarriage as well as the support you received in the hospital and beyond. Your experiences and wisdom will not be appreciated by everyone, so try not to take it personally if someone does not agree with your understanding of grief.

CARPE DIEM

Write your own definition of grief and mourning. Perhaps you can even put a picture or drawing to each word or definition. This will help you to actually see how your grief is different from your mourning.

47.

TURN TO CEREMONY

"Ceremony helps you know what to do when you don't know what to do."
— Unknown

- One of the reasons miscarriage can be so hard is that to others, it is an invisible loss. Even your close friends and family may not have known about the pregnancy, and those who did never "saw" the pregnancy. There may have been no baby to bury, no grave to visit, no photographs to cherish.

- When someone we love dies, we have a funeral to give shape and structure to the experience. The ritual of the funeral helps us acknowledge and embrace our loss and invites the community to join together in grief.

- You can still honor this baby and this loss with ceremony. Ceremony can be healing because it helps us embrace the reality of the loss. It gives us space to recall and share parts of our story. It is a forum for giving and receiving needed support.

- Ceremonies don't have to be extravagant. They can include a small circle of your friends or just your immediate family or a community of parents who have also experienced miscarriage. Candle lighting, tree planting, drumming, or gatherings where you create a memorial piece (like a scrapbook or art piece) can all be forms of ceremony. Your ceremony may also include an affirmation of your faith or spiritual values. In many bodies of faith there are remembering practices or remembering prayers that can also be incorporated into your ceremony.

- Invite your close friends and family to gather. You could hold the ceremony at a place of worship, a park, or a home. Consider including prayers, music, candle-lighting, and a meal afterward. Ask a clergyperson or someone you know who's a good public speaker to help plan and lead the ceremony.

CARPE DIEM
Talk to someone today about your ideas for a ceremony.

48.

ACKNOWLEDGE THE MULTITUDE OF LOSSES

"My life is about ups and downs, great joys and great losses."
— Isabel Allende

- Because of the miscarriage, you lost not only the pregnancy and a future precious child but also a part of yourself. Your child was made from part of you and was growing because of you. Many grieving parents say that after a baby dies, a part of them dies too.

- Since your miscarriage, you may have also experienced the loss of a sense of security. Many parents describe that they feel betrayed (this was not supposed to happen, after all) and unsafe (it was unexpected, and for some parents, the cause may still be unknown). You may no longer trust life in the same way you once did.

- One of the most difficult losses for grieving parents after a miscarriage is the loss of hopes and dreams for the future. You didn't get to know this child or watch her grow up. It's important to mourn the loss of what you envisioned and longed for.

- With miscarriage also often comes the loss of a sense of hope and joy for future pregnancies. Understandably, pregnancy loss makes people fearful of what could happen with the next pregnancy. Repeat miscarriage compounds this fear.

- Allowing yourself to acknowledge the many layers of loss that your miscarriage has brought to your life is vital. To move forward in your grief journey, outwardly acknowledging all the many losses that you are encountering is essential.

CARPE DIEM

Name your many losses out loud to someone who is able to just sit and listen without trying to "make it better." Describe openly and honestly the experiences you were most looking forward to with this baby that now cannot be. Put words to the future experiences or events that you'll grieve because of your miscarriage.

49.

WATCH FOR WARNING SIGNS

*"Obstacles can't stop you. Problems can't stop you.
Most of all, other people can't stop you. Only you can stop you."*
— J. Gitomer

- Understandably, when you are going through such a difficult time, it's easy to fall back on self-destructive behaviors as a way to get through. You may feel the pain of this baby's absence and want to fill the space with something that will help you escape the pain.

- What are your signs that you need extra help?

  Do you sleep too much, or perhaps you are not sleeping well at all?

  Are you using drugs or alcohol to self-treat your pain?

  Are you isolating yourself?

  Are you overeating or restricting your eating?

  Do you feel restless and anxious most of the time?

  Are you planning to physically harm yourself or someone else?

- Try to be honest with yourself, as these are all signals to you that you need to ask for help. If others approach you about any behaviors that concern them, please listen to them. They are standing on the outside of this and may be able to see trends that you cannot see.

- Seeing a grief counselor is probably a good idea if you had a history of substance abuse, depression, or anxiety prior to the miscarriage.

- If thoughts of hurting yourself or taking your own life have crossed your mind, even passively, talk to someone about your depression without delay and get the help you need and deserve.

CARPE DIEM

Acknowledging to ourselves that we have a problem may come only after we have started on a downward spiral emotionally or behaviorally. If someone suggests that you need help outside of your family and friendship circle, consider yourself lucky to be so well-loved and ask them to help you find someone to talk with.

50.

IDENTIFY SOMEONE YOU CAN COUNT ON

*"Friendship isn't about whom you have known the longest.
It's about who came and never left your side."*
— Unknown

- You may have many people whom you are absolutely sure care about you. But not all of these caring others are going to be good companions to you in grief.

- Someone who companions you in grief is able to bear witness to your emotional pain and allow your tears to flow without trying to stop you. She is willing to listen without giving you advice or telling you how you should feel. She is able to allow you to take this at your own pace instead of pulling you forward because she wants you to "get over" your grief sooner than your natural pace.

- Can you identify a person you know who is able to truly companion you during this time? If you can, reach out to this person today. Connecting with him and letting him know that you could use a companion on this journey may help you feel more anchored and hopeful right now.

- Though we would like to assume that everyone who loves us will be able to support us in this way, it's important to know that even very compassionate people sometimes find it hard to be present to others in grief.

- If any of your closest friends seem to have abandoned you, don't assume that you can't count on them. They probably need you to take the lead. Invite them to talk with you about your miscarriage. Invite this friend or family member to lunch, be candid about your feelings, and teach them directly how they can help.

CARPE DIEM
Today, reach out to the best helper you know and ask for her help.

51.

SET BOUNDARIES

"Setting boundaries is a way of caring for myself. It doesn't make me mean, selfish, or uncaring because I don't do things your way. I care about me, too."

— Christine Morgan

- Miscarriage is one of the most emotionally draining experiences that a couple can share. You had to say hello and goodbye to this baby within a short period of time.

- Especially if you are reading this soon after your miscarriage, you may find that your body lacks the energy to participate in activities you used to find pleasant. You may not even feel a desire to connect with others in the same ways that you have in the recent past. Your body, mind, and soul need time to recuperate.

- It's OK to say no when you are asked to attend an event, join a group, or spend time with friends. Saying no can be done politely but firmly. Let people know that you can't participate right now, but you appreciate that they asked.

- Of course, you don't want to say "no" forever. Find an event that seems low-key and plan to go. If you attend something and find it overwhelming, it's OK to excuse yourself and leave early. If you are fearful of people approaching you and having awkward conversations, be prepared with a response that lets others know that you need to set a boundary around the conversation. Say, "I'm not ready to talk about it yet. Today I want to just focus on being back to book club and seeing all of you again."

- Isolating yourself from friends or social groups over a long period can result in the loss of your support network and loneliness in your grief. If it begins to feel as if your grief is resulting in your missing out on life's most joyful celebrations—birthdays, weddings, performances by your children—this is a sign that you may be pulling inward too often. Finding a balance between being alone and being with others while you are grieving is vital.

CARPE DIEM

It can be difficult to set healthy boundaries for yourself. Take some time to consider what boundaries are absolutely necessary right now for you given that your energy level may be low. Take the things that you can off your plate to make room for your mind and body to begin the healing process.

52.

PREPARE TO ANSWER
UNCOMFORTABLE QUESTIONS

"Don't duck the most difficult problems.
That just ensures that the hardest part will be left when you are most tired.
Get the big one done—it's downhill from then on."

— Norman Vincent Peale

- What were once happy, even exciting questions to answer are now riddled with pain and can trigger high emotions. Which questions do you dread being asked? How will you answer them?

  Weren't you pregnant?

  Did you just have a baby?

  Where is your baby?

  What was wrong with the baby?

  Why did they make you deliver the baby?

  How many children do you have?

- After a miscarriage, some grieving parents are caught off-guard by the questions people will ask. In order to prepare for the inevitable, it may help to come up with standard responses that you can customize depending on whom you are talking to and in what situation. This may be something to talk about with your partner to find out what he or she plans to say to others. You and your partner may decide to answer such questions differently, but it is helpful to know how much information each of you is sharing when asked.

- Most grieving parents report that answering these questions gets easier and more natural over time. The more prepared you are to answer, the easier these uncomfortable moments will be.

CARPE DIEM

What would be the most difficult question someone could ask you about this loss? Take a moment to decide how you will answer it if you are asked.

53.

SHARE YOUR STORY

"Live your life from your heart. Share from your heart.
And your story will touch and heal people's souls."
— Melody Beattie

- The story of this pregnancy spans from the moment you were thinking about conceiving this child to right now in this moment. It is your story and it is a story that, when given a voice, will become a more integrated part of you rather than something that "happened to you."

- Acknowledging your loss of this baby is a painful, ongoing process that you will work on in doses over time. A vital part of dosing yourself is telling the story to others. Each time you tell the story, it becomes a little more real and more an integral part of you.

- Your "story" is the circumstances surrounding your miscarriage, your thoughts and feelings about the pregnancy, your hopes and dreams for the baby's life, as well as memories of learning you were pregnant, the days or weeks of the pregnancy, the miscarriage itself, and the sinking moment you learned that you would miscarry.

- Find the person or people who are able to really listen and will allow you to tell the story, over and over again with as much detail as you need, without jumping in, advising you, or judging how your story unfolded.

- You and your partner may find surprising comfort in telling each other what you remember about the process of conceiving, the pregnancy, and the miscarriage. You may each recall different things or remind one another of a detail that might be meaningful.

CARPE DIEM
Write down your story today in a journal or in the form
of a letter or email to someone else.

54.

TALK TO YOUR BABY

"If the others heard me talking out loud they would think that I am crazy.
But since I am not, I do not care."
— Ernest Hemingway

- If your baby were sitting with you, in your arms, and you could tell her how you are doing, what would you say? If you were able to tell her what you wished for her, what would you share? If you were able to say anything, what words would you express to her?

- Talking out loud to someone who is not here can feel strange at first. We aren't sure where they are or if they can hear us. For some parents, it's simply enough to know that it's possible that this child could hear them.

- When you do start talking, be open and share your deepest thoughts and feelings with her about yourself, your grief, your life, your other children, or your dreams.

CARPE DIEM
Write this baby a letter. Tell him what you thought
and felt during the pregnancy. Let him know what you hoped for
and what you will miss because he is not here.
Share this letter with your partner or someone who loves you.

55.

IGNORE HURTFUL ADVICE

"An apple a day will keep anyone away, if thrown hard enough."
— Unknown

- Sometimes well-meaning but misinformed family members or friends will say something that is hurtful to you.

- You may hear them say things like:

  I know how you feel.

  Your baby is in a better place.

  It's time to move past this and get on with your life.

  Keep your chin up.

  This is probably a blessing in disguise.

  At least you can still have other children.

  Think of all you have to be thankful for.

  Now you have an angel in heaven.

  It will be OK.

  You will feel better soon.

  You're strong. You will get over this.

  God wouldn't give you more than you can handle.

- Try not to take these misguided words of advice to heart. Such clichés are often offered because people don't know what else to say. While you know that these comments dismiss your pain and diminish the reality that this is a unique and significant loss, others are often not aware.

CARPE DIEM

The next time you hear one of these platitudes, try to hear the concern and empathy behind it instead of the literal words that are spoken.

56.

TAKE CARE OF YOU

---

*"As you consciously choose to give yourself the gifts of self-care,
they become an integral part of your rhythm and the vital tools
that you will tap into for the rest of your life."*

— Miranda J. Barrett

- Sometimes when we are in mourning we feel weighted down, dull, or muted. You may wonder if what you are feeling on the inside is somehow visible to others on the outside. If you find yourself feeling unattractive or dull, know that it's natural for your self-esteem to be affected by your grief.

- You may not be bothering with your appearance right now because you have low energy or it doesn't seem as important as it once did. You might be telling yourself, "It doesn't matter if I do my hair or get dressed to go out today. I just lost my baby. That's what matters." You are right. The grief in your heart needs your attention right now.

- Yet, part of good self-care and healing is practicing to love and value life again, including your physical life. Take a look in the mirror and compassionately reacquaint yourself with you. This doesn't mean you should be over-focused on your appearance or your physique. It just means that your broken heart isn't the only facet of your being that needs your attention right now.

- Your emotional state can and will change when you change your physical state. Smile for 30 seconds right now (a full 30 seconds). You can feel something change in you physically. Now, frown for 30 seconds, and you'll feel your emotional state change again. Smile one more time (to end with a smile!), and experience the remarkable ability you have to alter your emotional state with a simple shift of your physical self.

CARPE DIEM

Were you good at taking care of yourself before this loss?
If you were not, it will not feel natural to nurture yourself. Each day devote time (even 10 minutes) to yourself. You can do anything with this time. There is no pressure to engage in an activity or to spend money. This is just 10 minutes of "me" time that you gift to yourself each day. Why? Because you deserve to be taken care of!

57.

MAKE SLEEP A PRIORITY

"A good laugh and a long sleep are the best cures in the doctor's book."
— Irish proverb

- During the first few months after your miscarriage, you may notice that it's harder to fall asleep or that you tend to wake up during the night. Changes in your sleep patterns are normal and reflect your special needs right now.

- The longer you go without adequate sleep, the more your sleep deprivation will influence your mood, tolerance of others, and energy level. You may feel like you make up for poor sleep during the week by sleeping in on the weekends, but this is not as beneficial for your body as getting a consistent number of hours of sleep nightly.

- How many hours of sleep do you need to feel really rested? To achieve this number consistently, find a sleep-inducing technique that is effective for you and that you are willing to use nightly, such as

  - creating a relaxing reading ritual in bed.

  - taking a warm bath just before bed.

  - lighting a scented candle or incense that induces sleep, such as lavender.

  - listening to a theta wave soundtrack that promotes sleep.

  - drinking Sleepytime tea before bed.

CARPE DIEM
If you or someone in your family is having trouble sleeping,
create a sleep basket that anyone in the family can use.
Fill it with items and ideas that will help promote sleep. Some things
you might include: warm milk recipes, chamomile, dream catchers,
Sleepytime tea, a lavender sachet or scented candle, bath salts,
and a list of ideas for clearing the mind and relaxing the body.

58.

HONOR WHAT YOUR BODY NEEDS

"Your body is precious. It is your vehicle for awakening. Treat it with care."
— Buddha

- If you are the mother, your body has been through a great deal. You were pregnant. Your body was in the process of physical change. Your hormone levels rose and fell. You may have had a D&C or other procedure.

- Right now your body needs care and attention. Eat well, get ample sleep, and exercise lightly every day. Self-care is necessary for mourners, yet it's something many of us push aside.

- Sometimes women who miscarry feel angry with their bodies. But taking care of yourself physically is truly one way to fuel healing. Rest is especially important. Lay your body down two to three times a day for 20 minutes, even if you are not able to fall sleep. Hydrate your body. Dehydration can compound feelings of fatigue and disorientation. Try to move your body, even for just a five-minute walk a day.

- You may not trust your body and second-guess the signals it gives you now. After all, you may have thought your baby was developing and growing properly. Your body may not have been signaling to you that anything was wrong. Still, try to work on trusting what your body is telling you right now. When you are fatigued, rest. During grief, when we do not listen to our bodies, they will find a way to get our attention with a cold or an illness that forces us to slow down and rest.

CARPE DIEM

Identify which part of your physical needs you are neglecting most right now. Sleep? Nutrition? Relaxation? Exercise?
Move that need to the top of your priority list this week. Make a conscious effort to make sure that need is met every day over the next seven days.

59.

REACH OUT AND TOUCH

"We need 4 hugs a day for survival. We need 8 hugs a day for maintenance.
We need 12 hugs a day for growth."

— Virginia Satir

• When we're grieving, connection with other human beings is essential
to our healing. We can connect emotionally, but we can also connect
physically. Since ancient times, touch has been recognized as having
transformative, healing powers.

• After a miscarriage, your body may be hurting physically. You may
also be dismayed at or angry with your body. One way to begin to heal
your body and your relationship with it is, when you are ready, to allow
others to touch you.

• Have you hugged anyone lately? Held someone's hand? Put your arm
around another human being? You probably know several people who
enjoy hugging or physical touching. If you're comfortable with their
touch, encourage it in the weeks and months to come.

• Hug someone you feel safe with. Get a full-body massage. Walk arm in
arm with a friend.

CARPE DIEM
Sit on a sofa with your partner, legs extended and facing each other.
Give each other a foot massage as you talk about your loss.

60.

TRUST THAT YOU'RE NOT GOING CRAZY

"Feeling lost, crazy, and desperate belongs to a good life as much as optimism, certainty, and reason."
— Alain de Botton

- Grief and insanity can feel eerily similar sometimes. Do you feel like you can't concentrate or have wild thoughts and feelings coursing through you? Are you disorganized, confused, and easily distracted? Are you having intrusive, random thoughts about your miscarriage?

- These experiences are all common and normal in grief. Your mind is trying to understand and incorporate what happened, but it has trouble doing that while you're busy with the activities of daily life.

- Give your mind a much-needed break whenever possible. Sit and just think. Talk about your loss. Set aside as many daily activities as you can for now.

- You're not going crazy. You're grieving. Give attention to your grief and express it. Over time, that's what will help you feel more rational and "together" again.

CARPE DIEM

The next time you have that "going crazy" feeling, stop what you're doing and retreat to somewhere quiet. Focus on your breathing for a few minutes, then allow yourself to think and talk about your loss.

61.

IF YOU'RE HAVING DREAMS ABOUT THE BABY, SHARE THEM WITH SOMEONE CLOSE TO YOU

"Dreams are illustrations from the book your soul is writing about you."
— Marsha Norman

- It's not uncommon for couples who miscarry to dream about the baby or babies. This is a normal response to loss and grief.

- If your miscarriage was sudden and physically disturbing, you may have dreams that are upsetting, even violent. You may dream about your miscarriage. You may have seemingly unrelated nightmares. These dreams are your mind's way of attempting to process the reality of what happened.

- If you are consistently having nightmares following your miscarriage, I strongly suggest you see a professional counselor. You deserve to get help to sleep well as well as to understand what you might be able to do to help yourself convert your nightmares into dreams.

- On the other hand, you may have very happy, reassuring dreams about the baby. You may even feel you have been "visited" by him in your dreams. Perhaps he has told you that he's OK and that you'll be OK, too.

CARPE DIEM
Talking about your dreams—whether they're happy or sad—is another way to express your grief. Or you might consider starting a "dream journal" in which you record your dreams as soon as you wake up.

62.

CREATE A PERSONAL SANCTUARY JUST FOR YOU

*"Sanctuary, on a personal level, is where we perform
the job of taking care of our soul."*
— Christopher Forrest McDowell

- When grief, loss, and the need to mourn enter your life, you need a dedicated, safe space to call your own. You need a private territory where you can explore self-development and spiritual practices as well as read insightful books, meditate, journal, or simply contemplate the universe.

- Contemplation literally means to "create space for the divine to enter." It is good to acknowledge to yourself and to others how important a sanctuary space can be for your well-being.

- A personal sanctuary may be "your" seat or pew in your place of worship. It could be a garden in a park or a hiking path or a bench on the grounds of a retreat center. Sanctuaries are usually sanctified in some way to invite in and help you connect to the Divine. You can create a sacred space in your home by smudging the room or adorning it with items or furniture that help your mind focus on your spiritual self. You can say a special prayer or chant to designate that it is set apart from other rooms in your home as a sacred space.

- Use earthy paint colors, find a cozy chair, and consider installing a tabletop fountain in the space. You may want to be able to play gentle music that brings sounds into the room that remind you of spirit or the Divine (the ocean, gentle drops of rain, drumming, or flutes). Or maybe you want this space to be dedicated to silence. As author Thomas Moore wisely noted, "Silence allows many sounds to reach awareness that otherwise would be unheard."

CARPE DIEM

Consider what you want to feel when you are in your sanctuary—harmony, for example. Find colors for the walls, the sounds that you would like to vibrate through this space while you are present, and photos that resonate a meaningful message to you. Surround yourself with that message through colors, sounds, sights, and smells.

63.

TRUST IN YOURSELF

"Sometimes the purpose of a day is to merely feel our sadness, knowing that as we do, we allow whole layers of grief, like old skin cells, to drop off us."
— Marianne Williamson

- Allow yourself to think, feel, and do whatever you need to think, feel, and do to survive early on. Try to keep the judgments about how or what you are doing to a minimum. There is no specific way you are "supposed" to grieve, so when you find yourself saying, "I'm supposed to…," take a moment to remind yourself that what you are feeling is exactly what you need to be feeling. Give yourself permission to grieve *your* way. There is no single right way to grieve, no orderly stages you will go through, and absolutely no timetable.

- You know what is churning inside your heart, mind, and soul after your miscarriage. No one else can see or feel what you see and feel. Let your journey unfold as it does. And give yourself permission to grieve in your own unique way.

- If others judge you or try to direct your grief in ways that seem unhelpful or even hurtful, remind yourself that there is only one person who knows what is best. You are the only expert of your grief. You can choose to believe what they say, or you can believe in your own intuitive grief process. Others are often well-intentioned but may lack insight about how miscarriage impacts a person physically, socially, emotionally, cognitively, and spiritually.

CARPE DIEM

Instead of pushing yourself to do more, dedicate a time each day to being still. Do nothing but take care of yourself in some small way—lay your body down for 20 minutes, get a massage, take a long shower, watch a comedy, eat something that you love to eat.

64.

LET GO OF TENSION WITH A SIGH

*"Breathe. Let go. And remind yourself that this very moment
is the only one you know you have for sure."*
— Oprah Winfrey

- You can release tension and stress through your breath. When you take a deep breath in through your nose, filling your belly (not your chest), you can imagine that your breath is like a sponge soaking up tiny particles of tension that sit within you. When you are ready, release all of that tension you've gathered through an audible, outward sigh.

- Sighing is an easy way to release or let go of something you are holding onto. We are, in a way, accepting that there is something burdensome present in us and that we have the capacity to move it from the inside to the outside.

- For some, sighing is like a form of prayer more powerful than words. In the Bible, Romans 8 describes that when there are not words for our prayer, the spirits intervene and pray for us. Their prayer comes in the forms of sighs, sighs deeper than anything that can be expressed in words.

- Allow your body to sigh. Sigh deeply. Sigh whenever you are in a space where you feel comfortable sighing. With each sigh you are acknowledging through a conscious action that while you have the ability to control your breath, you are not in total control of your life.

CARPE DIEM
Right now, take a deep breath in and hold your breath for a count of five. Then with an open mouth (jaw dropped slightly), sigh, pushing that breath outward as loudly and deeply as you can. Do this slowly five times in a row. Do you feel as if you have emptied something from yourself?

65.

PROTECT YOURSELF FROM NEGATIVITY

"Dwelling on the negative simply contributes to its power."
— Shirley MacLaine

- When we experience a major loss or feel overwhelmed with stress in our lives, our natural instinct is to want to shut things down—shut people out, shut noises off, and shut out the chaos going on around us. In order to survive, our mind and body instinctually want to shut doors instead of opening them.

- Right now there is no need to surround yourself with unneeded noise or demanding people who take away energy rather than provide comfort or support. Negativity and stress is all around us; it may be very helpful to find ways to set good boundaries around yourself so that negative information does not keep coming at you.

- You might consider turning on the television less often or taking a hiatus from the daily news or newspaper. Violent videogames, movies with depressing storylines, and the dystopian books that are so popular right now may be things you want to eliminate for at least a few weeks. If there are people in your life who seem to always complain or focus on what is wrong rather than what is good in the world, minimize your contact with them for a bit. Going to places that are busy and chaotic, such as the mall or restaurants, may also be something you want to take a break from. Try it and see if your days feel less heavy when negative or depressing information is not coming at you.

- Spend time with people who have positive and warm energy. Spend more time in places where you know others are going to be sending you messages of hope, life, and light.

CARPE DIEM
Make a list of the sources of negativity in your life. How can you give yourself a break from these people, places, or experiences?

66.

LEARN SOMETHING NEW

"Life begins at the end of your comfort zone."
— Unknown

- Sometimes when we are grieving we feel stuck. We can feel depressed day after day, and the daily routine of our lives can seem joyless.

- If you feel stuck, try learning something new. When you direct your mind through learning, you are taking control of part of your life. The miscarriage you experienced has ripped away your sense of control. Regain a little piece of it by learning something new.

- What have you always wanted to learn but have never tried? Playing the guitar? Woodworking? Speaking French?

- Consider physical activities. Learning to play golf or doing karate have the added benefits of exercise.

CARPE DIEM
Get a hold of your local community calendar and sign up
for a class in something you have never tried before.

67.

FIND HELP ONLINE

"The internet is becoming the town square for the global village of tomorrow."
— Bill Gates

- The Internet has many interesting, informative, and, yes, healing resources for mourners.

- Families who've suffered a miscarriage can find affirmation for their profound sense of loss on sites like compassionatefriends.org, thesolacefoundation.org, and fertilityplus.com.

- You might also want to participate in an online support group on sites like miscarriage.supportgroups.com and dailystrength.org. Like face-to-face support groups, online versions can be extremely supportive and healing for couples after pregnancy loss.

- Facebook and other social media tools are another good option for some grieving couples. Remember, as long as you're reaching out, expressing, and sharing, you're actively mourning...which, over time, will lead to healing.

CARPE DIEM
Use your computer to search for some solace and compassion today.

68.

REMEMBER, EVEN ROCKS CRUMBLE WITH TOO MUCH WEIGHT

"I want to weep, she thought. I want to be comforted.
I'm so tired of being strong. I want to be foolish and frightened for once.
Just for a small while, that's all...a day...an hour."
— George R.R. Martin, *A Clash of Kings*

- In the face of loss, a common response is to try to buck up and stoically be a rock-solid source of support for others around you who are also grieving. If you are the person in your family who is taking on this role as the "rock," be aware that it will be difficult and even detrimental to sustain.

- Fathers are especially vulnerable to being the "rock" after a loss. Others may even encourage you to do this by saying, "Be strong for them" or "Your family is counting on you to carry them through this." Try not to let these statements misguide you into believing it's best to ignore your own grief or trauma. In a flight emergency, whose oxygen do you need to strap on first in order to help your child or partner who is sitting next to you? Your own! Making sure you are taking care of your grief first, in doses, is essential to supporting your family through this.

- Grief doesn't evaporate because we figure out how to set it aside. It waits for you to return, and if you don't, it will find a way to get your attention.

- It's natural to want to keep some solid ground while your family is going through this difficult time, but you can do this in ways other than emotional stoicism. Solid ground can be found by bringing structure into your home, being consistent with how you respond when your child or partner is actively mourning, following through on what you say, reminding your family that you are always someone they can count on, and making sure you are accessible when your family needs you.

CARPE DIEM

Redefine what it means to be "strong" during this grief journey. Take a minute to write down your definition and the actions that embody that definition. Make sure that at least once a week you do something that actively helps you express the grief you are carrying.

69.

FIND THE WORDS IN MUSIC

"Give sorrow words; the grief that does not speak
whispers the o'er-wrought heart and bids it break."
— William Shakespeare

- When we cannot find the words to express what we are feeling or thinking, it's amazing how music and lyrics have a way of saying what we need to, but cannot.

- Have you heard a song that reminds you of how you feel about your pregnancy or miscarriage? Is there a song that you listened to while you were pregnant that speaks to you? Is there a message that you want this baby to know (or others to know) that you were not able to give him the way you had planned?

- Find a song or songs that allow you to express the thoughts and feelings that are so jumbled inside of you right now. Make a playlist, and when you want to consciously set aside time and space to mourn, listen to your playlist and let your emotions surface.

CARPE DIEM

Since your miscarriage, have you happened upon a song that triggered deep emotion in you? Turning off the radio to avoid these "griefbursts" seems easier than feeling the pain they trigger. But these songs can be helpful in your grief journey. I encourage you to create a time each day or week and listen to them somewhere you can allow your grief to surface and flow from the inside of you out.

70.

FIND WAYS TO HONOR THIS BABY

"It hurts when you have someone in your heart but can't have them in your arms."
— Unknown

- Depending on the circumstances of your miscarriage, you may or may not have had a chance to see or spend time with the baby's body or to have a ceremony marking your loss. There is typically no grave or columbarium niche that forever memorializes this baby you loved.

- Regardless, you can still honor this loss and this baby. Consider making a donation in the baby's name to the March of Dimes or another organization that's important to you. Choose a date—perhaps the date of the miscarriage or the baby's due date—and do something special each year on that day.

- You can also honor this baby in a visible and permanent way. We've discussed how the invisibility and liminality of miscarriage makes it an extremely hard type of loss to think and talk about. Making it concrete often helps parents, families, and friends mourn and support one another. Here are some ideas:

  - Plant a tree in your yard and place a marker at its feet.

  - Buy a baby outfit and place it in a shadow box to hang on your wall.

  - Donate a book to your local or school library in your baby's name.

  - Buy or make a Christmas or holiday ornament that you will get out each year in remembrance of this baby.

  - Every year on the anniversary of your miscarriage, hang a special flag or wreath on your front door.

CARPE DIEM
Do something tangible today in honor of this baby.

71.

VOLUNTEER

"If you want to lift yourself up, lift up someone else."
— Booker T. Washington

- Consider honoring the baby you lost by helping others in your community. Volunteer at a senior center, an elementary school, a local hospital—someplace that supports your values and feels close to your heart.

- My friends Bonnie and Tony Redfern have started an annual run in their community of Fresno, California, in loving memory of their son Scott, who died suddenly in a tragic shop accident at school. Another couple I am close to, Nancy and Gary Zastrow, founded educational programs, support groups, and a newsletter in their town of Wausau, Wisconsin, following the suicide death of their beloved son, Chad. And my treasured friend Andrea Gambill started *Bereavement* magazine after an auto accident took the life of her darling daughter, Judy. All of these special people have helped countless others as a way to honor life and make sense of death.

- You might also consider helping others in your community who have lost a child to miscarriage. Look into starting a support group or annual fundraising event.

- If your schedule is too hectic, offer money instead of time. Make your donation in memory of the baby you lost.

CARPE DIEM

Call your local United Way and ask for some suggestions about upcoming events you could participate in or organizations you could help.

72.

TELL SOMEONE YOU LOVE HER

"Silent gratitude isn't much use to anyone."
— Gladys Browyn Stern

- This miscarriage may have made you very aware of how precious and important love is in this world. Love makes people smile, and the presence of love can help us through the most trying of times.

- Sometimes we love people but forget to put our feelings into words or actions. We don't say "I love you" as often as we could. We may believe that they already know, so there is no need to say it. We might assume they can feel it or see it through our actions, so it doesn't need to be spoken. Gifting these three words to another person—"I love you"—is a gentle reminder to them that whether they feel it or not, whether you've shown it or not, it's true.

- When they are spoken out loud to someone with whom we have a strong connection—our child, our spouse, our parents, our lifelong friend—these three simple words take on a deep spiritual meaning. Yet we sometimes fail to see the significance of saying these words until it's too late.

- Whom in your life would you like to hear more "I love yous" from? Who do you know in your mind who loves you but doesn't say the words? Even if you are not always receiving the words, make it a priority to say them. Let them hear it come from you so there is no doubt, no assumption, just acknowledgment that love exists.

CARPE DIEM
Call someone you love right now and give her the
lasting gift of telling her you love her.

73.

ACKNOWLEDGE WHEN YOU ARE FEELING LOST

"Not all those who wander are lost."
— J.R.R. Tolkien

- Death is not what you were preparing for. You were preparing for life! You may have started picking names, reading up on childbirth, working on the baby's room, or planning a maternity leave.

- Grief-ridden is not where you expected to be today, and mourning this loss is not what you expected to be doing. What your body and mind were expecting was to be getting ready for the baby's birth then caretaking and nurturing the child.

- The sudden change in reality may leave you feeling lost. You may experience many moments of feeling at loose ends, unsure what you are supposed to do now.

- Acknowledge out loud to your partner and to yourself when you are feeling "lost." It will help you to stop and take a moment to dose yourself with the painful reality that you must now make new plans. Express your pain (moan, sigh, cry, talk) as you engage in a task or action that you feel is meaningful to you. These moments of feeling lost are a natural part of this grief journey. Be compassionate with yourself as you wander through the early weeks after your miscarriage.

CARPE DIEM
If you're feeling lost, stop what you're doing and take a break. Go for a walk, meditate, or lay your body down for a rest.

74.

ALLOW FOR UNFINISHED BUSINESS

"Courage is being afraid and going on the journey anyhow."
— John Wayne

- Loss often brings about feelings of unfinished business. Time was something you didn't get with this baby. There were so many things you didn't get to say, so many things that you were unable to do, because of your miscarriage.

- Is there something you wanted to say to this baby? Is there something that happened during the pregnancy that you feel regretful about? Is there an action you wish you could take right now, if you had the chance to be with this baby just one more hour or one more day?

- Allow yourself to think about and feel the emotions related to all that feels "unfinished." Your "if onlys" may never fully be resolved in your mind and heart, but if you permit yourself to put them outside of yourself (to give voice to them, to mourn them), you will be able to reconcile even those that you are not able to complete.

CARPE DIEM

If you carry any feelings of unfinished business about this pregnancy or this baby, tell someone about them today.

75.

SIMPLIFY

"Life is really simple, but we insist on making it complicated."
— Confucius

- There is no better time than now to take stock of what's really important in your life. Once you do this, you may find that it is easy to discard what is weighing you down or not serving you.

- As you are doing the essential work of grief and mourning, it's easy to become overwhelmed by all of the other tasks, demands, and commitments you have—keeping your relationship healthy, taking care of other children you may have, meeting demands at work, keeping your home up, fulfilling your obligations to committees you're on, helping others who need you. If you can rid yourself of any extraneous burdens, you'll have more time for your family and for healing.

- What is overburdening you right now? Have your name taken off junk-mail lists. Hire someone to clean your home. Stop attending any optional meetings you don't look forward to or are unnecessary right now. Ask someone to help you with meals or childcare. Let your friends know that you will need to take a hiatus from PTA, carpool, or your neighborhood book club if you are part of these. Ask a friend to help you with running errands, getting groceries, paying bills, etc.

- Often your family and friends would like to help but don't know how or what to do. Make a list of all the things that need to get done in a typical day then choose at least three of these that you can ask someone else to help with for the next month or so.

CARPE DIEM
Have a family meeting and take stock of your family
activities calendar. Ask everyone present which activities
they truly want to continue and which they would be happier without.
Make cuts where appropriate. Maybe you can even fill in some
of the extra time you all have with a little vacation get-away.

76.

PREPARE YOURSELF FOR THE HOLIDAYS

"For many people, holidays are not voyages of discovery,
but a ritual of reassurance."
— Philip Andrew

- Perhaps you were looking forward to the holidays after this baby was born. Now that things didn't turn out the way you were imagining, you may feel particularly sad and vulnerable during family gathering like Thanksgiving, Christmas, Hanukkah, and Easter.

- It is common in our society for people to overextend themselves during the holidays. Try not to put pressure on yourself to do all of the shopping, baking, entertaining, and mailing of holiday cards this year if you are not up for it.

- Sometimes participating in traditional holiday rituals can feel comforting after a significant loss, and sometimes it does not. Continue them only if they feel good to you; consider creating new traditions if that feels better.

- If you are able to find a way to make remembering your baby part of your holiday ritual, this may help you feel the holidays are more fulfilling. For example, you could decorate a small tabletop tree each year at Christmas in honor of your baby. Or purchase a special ornament or make a special dish (angel food cake) that can be a way for your family, without words, to know that you are all thinking of the baby who is not here to celebrate this special day with you.

CARPE DIEM
What's the next major holiday? Make a plan right now and let those you usually spend the day with know what you are planning.

77.

DEMONSTRATE YOUR FAITH

"Faith is taking the first step even when you don't see the whole staircase."
— Martin Luther King, Jr.

- Above all, mourning is a spiritual journey of the heart and soul. Miscarriage can give rise to profound spiritual yearnings and chaos. You may find that this loss has invited you to examine your beliefs about death and develop an understanding of where God or your higher power fits within your suffering.

- If you have faith or a spiritual side, express it in ways that seem congruent with who you are and what you are going through right now.

- Attending church or your place of worship, reading religious texts, and praying are a few conventional ways to express spirituality. If meditating, hiking, or spending time alone in nature resonate more with your spiritual needs, make time each week for those activities.

- For many grieving parents, having faith means holding the belief that they will one day see their baby. This belief alone, whether the reconnection will be in heaven, through reincarnation, or in a less-defined afterlife, makes getting through the days more bearable for some parents.

CARPE DIEM
Find a quote or two on faith that resonate with you and place them somewhere you will see them often—as computer screensavers, near your bathroom mirror, or maybe on the dashboard of your car.

78.

GROUND YOUR THOUGHTS WITH A TOUCHSTONE

"Be curious, not judgmental."
—Walt Whitman

- A touchstone can be a very useful tool during your grief journey. Touchstones can be used to help you set an intention or to bring a behavior into consciousness, a behavior that you want to reinforce in your everyday life.

- Let's say that you want to "be kind" no matter how others respond to your loss. When you are deciding how to react in a difficult situation, such as when someone says something inappropriate or dismisses the significance of your loss, you might be tempted to explode in anger. But when you focus on your touchstone, you pause before the anger erupts. You consider your "be kind" mantra and instead decide that an angry outburst would be counterproductive and hurtful to you as much as it would be hurtful to the other.

- I suggest that you literally carry a stone in your pocket to remind yourself of an intention you would like to realize. Whenever you're feeling your grief or struggling with a thought or feeling, put your hand in your pocket and hold the stone. Remind yourself that you want your response to come from a place of "kindness" if that is your intention. The stone's smooth surface will help center you and return you to your place of conscious living.

CARPE DIEM
Go to a specialty shop to purchase a rock with a meaningful word or phrase on it that touches your heart, such as "patience," "gratitude," "hope," or "connection." Or make a touchstone using a rock from your own backyard.

79.

COMMUNICATE WITH YOUR PARTNER ABOUT YOUR SEX LIFE

"I wonder if this is how people always get close:
they heal each other's wounds; they repair the broken skin."

— Lauren Oliver

- After a miscarriage, couples often struggle with how and when to continue their sex lives. One partner may be consumed with grief or feel so completely misunderstood that sex is the last thing on his or her mind.

- Beyond the waiting period that is recommended by doctors after a miscarriage (which will depend on the specific circumstances of your miscarriage), couples struggle around how and when to reengage sexually. The meaning of sex and the act of sex can take on a whole new meaning.

- Not always, but often, women are slower to feel ready to embrace intimacy again, while grieving men crave the pleasure and escape of sex. Both feelings are understandable and normal. There is no right way to handle this; there is only the need for open communication about it.

- If one partner wants to start having sex again and the other does not, it's important to talk openly about this reality. It is also critical to talk about why it is not wanted or why the timing is not right, so that assumptions are not being made by either person. Insisting or guilting your partner into anything he or she is not ready for will only breed resentment that will come out in other ways in the relationship.

- Be prepared for lovemaking to be more emotional in the early weeks and months after your miscarriage. Emotions are high and there is new sensitivity around connection, love, and intimacy.

- Eventually, most couples settle back into their normal sexual pattern. If you don't see this happening in your relationship or are unhappy with your sex life, it may help to work with a couples counselor.

CARPE DIEM

Talking about sex can be difficult or embarrassing for some couples. If you are having a hard time talking about it, perhaps find some other ways of communicating about sexual wants and needs. Try writing each other notes or reading a book on intimacy together.

80.

WRITE A LETTER TO
YOUR HIGHER POWER

"Babies are bits of stardust, blown from the hand of God."
— Barretto

- Sometimes expressing our thoughts and feelings on paper (in a letter, card, journal, or notebook) helps us to understand them better. When we can remove them from inside of our minds and actually see them in front of us, we can begin to take a different view. Sometimes, free-flowing writing can reveal a great deal about where we are struggling the most.

- If you were to write out your thoughts and feelings about your miscarriage to your "higher power," to whom would you address it and what would you say? Take a moment to write a brief letter now. Express how you feel in this moment. Consider the following prompts:

  Right now, my relationship with you is...

  Right now, when I think about my life I believe...

  Right now, my journey through grief feels...

  Right now, my hopes for the future are...

- You might also find it helpful to write notes of gratitude to those people who were or continue to be supportive of you at this time, including doctors, hospital staff, friends, family, and neighbors.

CARPE DIEM

Take a moment to reflect on how your higher power fits into your everyday life. How do you connect with that which you refer to as your higher power—through prayer, attending church, reading scripture, meditation, yoga, hiking in nature, stargazing etc.? Whatever ways you feel you reach your higher power, take 15 minutes today and spend time contemplating something bigger than yourself.

81.

DON'T BE CAUGHT OFF-GUARD BY GRIEFBURSTS

"Each of us has his own rhythm of suffering."
— Roland Barthes

- Heightened periods of sadness often overwhelm us when we are in the midst of grief.

- These bursts of sadness, which sometimes feel uncontrollable, seem to come of out nowhere. When they catch you off-guard, especially if you are unaware that they are normal and natural, they can be frightening and painful. But if you expect them as a natural part of your day or week, they may not be quite so overwhelming. You may actually be able to feel them coming on and have a plan for where you would like to go to allow the "burst" to surface.

- Even long after your miscarriage (a year or two or more), something as simple as a sound, a smell, or phrase can bring on a griefburst.

- Allow yourself to experience griefbursts without shame or self-judgment, no matter where and when they occur. Even if you or those around you don't understand what brings one to the surface, it's there and it is asking to be released. Most of the time, it's only uncomfortable for others because they don't know what to do to stop it. If only they knew that the thing to do is to welcome it, these moments would be much easier for everyone. If you feel more comfortable, retreat to somewhere private when these strong feelings surface.

CARPE DIEM

If you can recall your most recent griefburst, take a moment to write about it in a journal or an email. Identify what triggered the emotion (an object? event? song?). Make note of how you feel now about your expressiveness during that griefburst. If you are ashamed of how it unfolded—how you sounded, how you looked, take a moment and imagine that you were watching someone else behave the same way. What might you have said to him to assure him that it was not only natural but a necessary part of his grief journey?

82.

EXPECT GRIEF AT MILESTONES

"For the rest of my life, I will search for moments full of you."
— Unknown

- As we've discussed, grief never ends. Instead, your loss becomes a part of the story of your life.

- You will find that your grief over this miscarriage will flare up here and there long into the future. If you have other children, you may feel your grief on their birthdays or milestones like their graduations or weddings. If you go on to have another baby, you may be more at risk for postpartum depression, because the joy of the birth and healthy baby are also a reminder of the baby you never got to hold.

- Griefbursts on anniversaries and special occasions will probably become part of your new normal. Expect them. Embrace them. Feel them then let them go.

CARPE DIEM
Tell a special friend about griefbursts and ask her if you can call on her whenever one flares up.

83.

UNDERSTAND THE CONCEPT
OF RECONCILIATION

*"We can never obtain peace in the outer world
until we make peace with ourselves."*

— Dalai Lama

- You may have heard others reassure you that you will "recover from," "get over," "move past," or "accept" your loss of this baby. What many well-intentioned family and friends may not understand is that these words imply that your grief is an illness that must be cured. They also assume an eventual return to the way things were before your miscarriage. Neither of these are true. You are not ill. Your heart is broken and you are torn apart by this loss. You are not the same person today as you were before your miscarriage.

- You are forever changed by this loss. You are becoming a new you.

- This does not mean you will live in misery. Remember, when you allow yourself to actively mourn, you not only heal, but you transform as you move through to the other side of your grief. You don't recover from your loss, but you become reconciled to it. Your life can potentially be deeper and more meaningful in the future.

- When you have reconciled your grief, the sharp pangs of sorrow soften, the constant painful memories subside. A renewed interest in the future begins to overtake the natural obsession with the past and the loss. You experience more happy than sad in your days. You begin to set new goals and work toward them. You bond with other people and develop close relationships with others again, less fearful of losing them. You experience life again.

CARPE DIEM

Explore your understanding of reconciling your grief. What will your life look like once you have reconciled your grief? What will be in your life that is not present now? What will you feel that you do not feel now? What will you want that you do not want now?

84.

GET AWAY FROM IT ALL

"To travel is to take a journey into yourself."
— Danny Kaye

- Sometimes it takes a change of scenery to help us find perspective.

- New people and places help us see our lives and losses from a new vantage point and can assist us in our search for meaning.

- Often, getting away from it all means leaving civilization behind and retreating to nature. But it can also mean temporarily abandoning your environment and spending time in one that's altogether different.

- Even when you can't go far away, you can still "get away from it all" every few hours by getting up, walking around, looking out the window, and getting a drink of water. Take a reflective "time out" for several minutes.

- Visit a different city or a foreign country. Go backpacking in the wilderness. Spend a weekend at a monastery or somewhere altogether unlike your usual places.

CARPE DIEM

Plan a trip to somewhere far away. Ask a friend to travel with you. Just don't do this too soon; running away is not the same as getting away.

85.

THINK ABOUT WHAT COMES NEXT

"All that we are is the result of what we have thought."
— Buddha

- While you should not set a particular time and course for your healing, it may help you to give thought to other life goals that you would like to reach over the coming months. When we are grieving we are often focused on what happened or how we are going to make it through today. We can quickly lose sight of what comes next, and what kind of future we want to create for ourselves or our family.

- Your goals do not have to be enormous. Even simple goals like traveling to a place that you've always wanted to experience, learning to do something you've always been fearful to try, or reading a book that you would enjoy can help you find hope.

- Take a few moments to write a list of short-term goals, goals that you can see yourself doing over the next two months. Perhaps some of the goals could have to do with mourning activities, like organizing a ceremony or taking a yoga class that centers on energetically moving your grief through a series of poses.

- At the same time, write out a few long-term goals about which, a year from now, you would like to be able to say, "I did that!" Reflect on the goals you had as a child or something you dreamed of after college. Be both realistic and compassionate with yourself as you consider what is feasible or what feels right rather than goals that will only add stress to your days.

- Read through your list each day, just to remind yourself of the direction you want to move. Place a copy of your list in a location where you will be able to see it and be reminded that you are giving attention to what comes next.

CARPE DIEM
Transform your list of goals from words into pictures. Draw, use magazines, find photos online if you need to. What do you actually see in your future? Create a visual reminder of what comes next.

86.

MOVE YOUR GRIEF TO GRATITUDE WITH YOGA

*"You can clutch the past so tightly to your chest that it
leaves your arms too full to embrace the present."*

— Jan Glidewell

- Yoga is a 3,000-year-old tradition that originated in India. Today there are tens of thousands of yoga studios that teach a variety of different styles. The primary goal in yoga is to integrate mind, body, and spirit, creating a "wholeness" or "oneness" in your entire being.

- A mixture of physical postures, meditation, and deep breathing, yoga serves to strengthen the body physically, mentally, emotionally, and spiritually, which can be extremely beneficial as you move through your grief. In yoga, as you move you can actually move the energy in your body by positioning it in certain poses as well as breathing appropriately as you flow through from one posture to the next.

- All yoga postures involve what are called *pranayamas*, or breathing purifications, that enhance inner tranquility. How you breathe during each movement influences the flow of your energy as you transition from pose to pose. Yoga encourages you to breathe deeply to bring oxygen to your cells and exhale slowly to rid the body of toxins. Long, slow deep breaths can help center you and remind you to be present and one with your body. Yoga breathing infuses your body with *prana*, or energy.

- Some yoga studios offer workshops that incorporate body work that is focused on integrating any unhealed energies often associated with grief (shame, rejection, anger, abandonment). Standing balancing poses and back-bending poses that stimulate the thymus gland and begin to open up the heart and chest are often incorporated into this work.

CARPE DIEM
Create an action plan to sign up to take an introduction to yoga class. Get
online right now and Google "yoga studios" to find locations near you.
If you are more advanced, find a class that will allow you to continue to
expand your yoga practice beyond where you are.

87.

BRING IN MORE LIGHT

"I will love the light for it shows me the way,
yet I will endure the darkness because it shows me the stars."
— Og Mandino

- Light is illuminating. It helps us see our way. It represents hope. It is the sign of a new day. Darkness can be just the opposite. It obstructs our vision and sometimes makes us feel afraid and hopeless. But even small amounts of light can help dispel those fears.

- Ask any child who is afraid of the dark and he will tell you that what helps is to bring light into his room. If you are feeling like you are in the darkness (and many grieving parents do feel this), make a conscious effort to bring more light into your space.

- Find creative and unique ways to light up the darkness you are feeling in your life space right now. Even when it's soft, light can be comforting, like a beacon in the night.

    - Buy nightlights for your hallways and other rooms.
    - Put candles in different rooms and light them when you are spending time in those areas.
    - Repaint walls with a lighter color to brighten up your space.
    - Keep your blinds and curtains open.
    - Purchase a lava lamp or unique lamp to be placed somewhere in your home.
    - Find a neon sign and find a way to add this to your décor.

CARPE DIEM

Take an afternoon and go nightlight shopping. You can find a variety of nightlights, from stained glass to ceramic to seashells to pressed dried flowers. Pick one out for your master bedroom and perhaps one to give as a gift in memory of your child.

88.

LAUGH

"Laughter is the language of the soul."
— Pablo Neruda

- Humor is one of the most healing gifts of humanity. Laughter restores hope and assists us in surviving the pain of grief.

- Don't fall into the trap of thinking that laughing and having fun are somehow a betrayal of the baby you lost. Laughing doesn't mean you don't still long for this baby. Laughing doesn't mean you aren't in mourning.

- You can only embrace the pain of your loss a little at a time, in doses. In between the doses, it's perfectly normal, even necessary, to love and laugh.

- I've heard it said that laughter is a form of internal jogging. Not only is it enjoyable, it is good for you. Studies show that smiling, laughing, and feeling good enhance your immune system and make you healthier. If you act happy, you may even begin to feel some happiness in your life again.

CARPE DIEM
Today, find time to watch a sitcom, funny movie, or stand-up comic on Netflix. Better yet, watch with your partner.

89.

TAKE IN THE SUN

"The sun illuminates only the eye of the man but shines into the eye and the heart of the child."

— Ralph Waldo Emerson

- The sun is a powerful symbol of life and renewal. It exudes warmth and light, which are both helpful to those who feel they are in the darkness of grief.

- When was the last time you watched the sun rise? Do you remember being touched by its beauty and power?

- Plan an early morning breakfast or walk in a location where you can see the sun rise. Hike to the top of a hill or a nearby lake where you can sit on a blanket and experience the dawn of a new day. Have coffee on a patio where you can see the sun rise. Sometimes you may have trouble sleeping and may be up early anyway. Invite a friend to share the rising sun with you.

- Watching the day begin like this could be emotional for you. The sunrise signifies newness, which is what you expected to experience with the birth of your baby. It's OK if emotion is part of your sunrise experience. Continue to watch as you let your emotions pour out.

CARPE DIEM

Invite a friend on an early morning drive. Choose a fitting destination for watching the sun rise. Pack a brunch—hot coffee and fresh fruit, perhaps. Take a photograph of your sunrise so that you can be reminded of it on other days when you are not so fortunate to witness it in person.

90.

EXPRESS YOUR GRIEF THROUGH ART

"Art washes away from the soul the dust of everyday life."
— Pablo Picasso

- The visual arts have a way of making us see the world anew. In art we can find new perspectives, new ways of looking at ourselves, our relationships, and our surroundings. Art comes in so many forms. What kind of art do you enjoy?

- After a significant loss, we tend to spend more time in contemplation, and sometimes visual arts invite us to do just that. Perhaps a visit to an art gallery, a museum, a sculpture garden, a photography exhibit, or a botanical garden would be refreshing for you.

- If you find a piece of art that reminds you of the baby you were expecting or your parent-child connection, buy it and display it in a place that feels right to you.

- If you are creative, why not try to create a work of art yourself? Attend a watercolor or calligraphy class. Making pottery is something almost everyone enjoys. It's tactile and messy and whimsical. Cocktails-and-canvas classes are a way for families to spend time together and engage their artistic side.

CARPE DIEM
Buy some paints, brushes, and a canvas. With your whole family or by yourself, paint the feelings you are filled with right now about your miscarriage. They may be feelings of peace, sorrow, anger, regret— or a mixture of many emotions. Don't worry about your artistic abilities; just let your hand and imagination take the lead.

91.

CONTEMPLATE THE UNIVERSE

*"There is only one corner of the universe you can be
certain of improving, and that's your own self."*

— Aldous Huxley

- We are a small part of a much larger entity. You may know very little about the universe we live in, or you may have an expansive awareness of it. Regardless of your knowledge base, the universe can be an amazing, awe-inspiring topic of contemplation, especially during a time when you are searching for meaning in your life.

- Stargazing can be a relaxing, renewing activity. Taking in the darkness, the solitude, the constellations, and the depth of the space around the earth can foster frank conversations about the circle of existence, the meaning of life, and the experience of death.

- Do you have a telescope? If so, get it out and refresh your memory on how to use it. If you don't have one, gazing at the night sky with the naked eye can be equally awe-inspiring.

- Invite someone (a friend, your children, someone who knows more about the universe than you) to take a drive in the country where city lights won't obscure the starlight or a night hike to the top of a small mountain. Bring a blanket so that you can lie on your backs and stargaze in comfort.

- If you are unable to find the right place because you live in a city, make a plan to visit your local planetarium and contemplate what is much larger than yourself. What does that mean to you? Reflect on how your miscarriage fits into this larger perspective of life and the universe we are a small part of.

CARPE DIEM

Look it up online or visit your local library to gather information
about when the next interesting cosmic event will happen
(such as a meteor shower, a blue moon, or an eclipse). Invite someone
to accompany you to a good viewing spot and stay up to watch
something that may only occur once in your lifetime.

92.

EXPRESS YOUR CHILDLIKE SELF

"There is no point in being grown up if you can't be childish sometimes."
— Doctor Who

- Sometimes you will need a reprieve from the sadness and reality that this baby died. Wouldn't it be amazing to be able to go back to a time when you were a kid, when you were innocent and carefree, before loss touched your heart?

- It is the nature of children to live in the moment and appreciate what is right in front of them. They know how to be present and enjoy "right now." All of us would benefit from inviting a little more childlike energy into our lives.

- The beauty of it is, you can do this! All you need to do is create the time and decide the what and where and with whom you'd like to express your childlike self.

- How long has it been since you rode your bike without having an agenda of exercise, chewed bubblegum, fed the ducks in a pond, laid on your back in the grass, went wading in a stream, ran through a sprinkler, shuffled barefoot across freshly mown grass, had a snowball fight, or built a sandcastle?

- Give yourself permission to do something childlike today, such as blow bubbles, jump rope, learn to yo-yo, visit a toy store, fly a kite, or climb a tree.

- If you have children, invite them to join you for your play date. If you don't, ask a friend's child, your partner, or a friend who can take her adult hat off and let inhibitions go.

CARPE DIEM
Right now, leave your inhibitions behind. What are one or
two of your favorite childhood activities? Schedule these into your week.
You deserve this "time out" from your grief.

93.

WHEN AND IF EITHER OF YOU IS READY, TALK WITH YOUR PARTNER ABOUT TRYING AGAIN

"Everything you want is on the other side of fear."
— Jack Canfield

- You may not want to try to have another baby. But if and when you do, be open and communicative with your partner.

- At least 85 percent of women who miscarry go on to have normal pregnancies and births. Many, many families with healthy, happy children experienced miscarriage somewhere along the way.

- Still, taking time to heal physically (for the mom) as well as emotionally/ spiritually (for both partners) after this loss is essential before trying again. If you do not openly and honestly mourn your grief over this miscarriage before "moving on," you will carry it with you. Carried grief creates insidious ongoing problems, such as difficulties with trust and intimacy, depression, anxiety, and substance abuse.

- Know that this loss will always be a part of your life and the new, changed you you are becoming.

CARPE DIEM

If and when the conversation about trying again arises,
be compassionate and honest with your partner. You are each
entitled to your own thoughts and feelings about this, but you
cannot proceed until both of you are ready.

94.

REUNITE AND RECONNECT

"Nothing is more important than reconnecting with your bliss.
Nothing is as rich. Nothing is more real."
— Deepak Chopra

- Throughout our lives, we often lose contact with the people who've touched us, helped us grow in some way, or made us feel loved and valued.

- Experiencing a tragic loss can make us realize that keeping in touch with people who bring a smile to our face is well worth the effort it takes.

- Whom have you loved or admired but haven't spoken with for a long time? Is there a mentor, a teacher, a childhood friend, or a previous neighbor that you have disconnected with over the years?

- Think about a person who made a difference in your life and take a moment to find a way to reconnect with her. Send her a Facebook message, drop a card in the mail, buy her a small gift, write an email, shoot her a text. Try to be open with her about what prompted you to reconnect and why she has been on your mind during this time of sadness in your life.

CARPE DIEM
Spend time today adding friends to your Facebook or LinkedIn pages.
Find friends to follow on Twitter or Instagram that you haven't
connected with in a while. Reconnecting with people you have lost
touch with and re-inviting them into your life in small ways could be
helpful. Perhaps it's a person from your past who will "get" what you are
experiencing and turn out to be the best companion to you in grief.

95.

ENVISION

*"Deep, unspeakable suffering may well be called a baptism,
a regeneration, the initiation into a new state. Suffering can be likened
to a baptism—the passing over the threshold of pain and grief
and anguish to claim a new state of being."*

— George Elliot

- Tap into the power of visualization by dedicating time to picturing your best possible life.

- Close your eyes and visualize yourself living fully and joyfully. Where are you? What are you doing? Whom are you with?

- The powerful thing about visualizing your life after loss is that you see your desired future from the imperfect place and person you are today. You are the scarred and grieving you—someone who has been changed by loss and will be changed by more losses in the future. But despite all of the loss and the heartache, you can still see all the love and joy waiting for you if you only have the courage to envision it and head toward it.

- Envision your desired future then set off to get there.

CARPE DIEM

Make a vision board. Gather up old magazines and/or look online
and find images that capture the places and activities and feelings
you want to incorporate into your future.

96.

RECONFIGURE YOUR LIFE

"It is only possible to live happily ever after on a day-to-day basis."
— Margaret Bonnano

- When death and loss enter our life in any form, it has a way of making us rethink how we prioritize our days, interact with others, and spend our time.

- Have you considered what you give priority to? What gives your life meaning? Who are the people you want to spend time with? What are the activities you want to spend your valuable time doing? What doesn't give your life meaning that you still spend time on? What steps do you need to take to spend more of your time on the aspects of life that bring you a sense of meaning, purpose, and satisfaction?

- Now may be the time to reconfigure your life. After loss, we are less fearful and doubtful about our ability to reconfigure. Some people change careers, go back to school, begin volunteering, start a non-profit, reach out to others through a blog, or focus their time on deepening their relationship with people they love. What would your life look like reconfigured?

- Many grieving parents talk about how they can no longer tolerate being around people who come across as shallow, egocentric, or mean-spirited. It's OK to let friendships that are not serving you well come to an end. Instead, use your energy and time connecting with people who share your new outlook on living a meaningful life.

CARPE DIEM
Happiness is something everyone seems to be searching for.
But do you recognize happiness when it's in front of you?
Complete this sentence so that you can begin to give some of your
attention to thoughts outside of this loss.

For me, happiness is…

97.

BE PURPOSEFUL IN EVERYTHING YOU DO

"Chase away sorrow by living."
— Melissa Marr

- Do you think that you can make things happen by first creating them in your mind? The "Law of Attraction" (as it is sometimes called) has gained a lot of attention in recent years. If you believe that what you focus on will grow, why not do more things "on purpose" so that you create the life you most desire?

- For example, what if you lived with one of the following intentions over the next week?

  I intend to live in the present moment today.

  Today, I will set my intention to hold a child's hand or give her a hug so that she feels loved.

  My intention for the day will be to be direct and honest with everyone I see about what I need from them as I mourn the loss of this baby.

- When we live with awareness and intention, we are living on purpose. For example, if you set your intention to mourn well and heal, that is the direction your day will take. If you move forward each day embracing hope—even as you also embrace your pain—you are living a life that is purposefully centered on healing your grief.

- With a daily intention you will bring awareness into all of your interactions. Your intentional thoughts will create intentional actions. When you do this, you will experience a sense of control over at least some aspects of your destiny.

CARPE DIEM

Today set your intention for the coming month. With what attitude do you intend to wake up and enter the day? How do you intend to mourn so that you can learn to love and live well again?

98.

SHARE WHAT YOU'VE LEARNED

"You must be the change you wish to see in the world."
— Mahatma Gandhi

• Since your miscarriage, if you've connected with others and mourned well, you've learned a lot. You've learned what's helpful and what's not after a miscarriage. You've learned how to cope and how to heal.

• Others in your life and your community could be helped by what you've learned. Reach out to them. If you learn of other couples who experience miscarriage, send them a compassionate note of understanding and hope.

• Maybe you're also in a position to work with your local hospital to improve miscarriage care. How are couples who've miscarried treated at the hospital? How are they supported emotionally? What options are they given for disposition of the tissue or body? These are all things that, with the efforts of someone who's been there, could probably be improved. Or what if you started a program in which volunteers made keepsake blankets for all families who miscarried? What a gift that would be to future families who suffer miscarriage!

CARPE DIEM
In some small way today, share what you've learned about miscarriage with someone else who is struggling.

99.

SAY GOODBYE

*"If I had a single flower for every time I think of you,
I could walk forever in my garden."*
— Claudia Adrienne Grandi

- You never got to say a proper hello to this baby. I am so sorry about that. But if you have openly, honestly, and fully mourned your loss of this baby, you have, in essence, said a sort of hello. You have looked your thoughts and feelings about the pregnancy, the baby, and your miscarriage full in the face and you have expressed them. You have acknowledged your loss and worked on the six needs of mourning. You have begun to feel the caress of reconciliation.

- Now that you've said this hello, you can say goodbye. When we say goodbye to someone we love, we are not ending our relationship with them because love does not end. But we are converting our relationship with them from one of presence to one of memory.

- When you are ready, say goodbye to this baby. You will always love him or her. You will always remember him or her. You will always grieve for him or her. But you are ready to commit your energies and attention to the present and the future.

CARPE DIEM
When you are ready, write a goodbye note to this baby.

100.

EMBRACE YOUR TRANSFORMATION

*"Sometimes a breakdown can be the beginning of a kind of breakthrough,
a way of living in advance through a trauma that prepares
you for a future of radical transformation."*
— Cherríe Moraga

- You may find that you are changing emotionally and spiritually as a result of your grief journey. It may feel as if your insides have been shaken up or torn apart and that slowly they are falling back into different places. Your grief journey may be completely transforming, altering what once was into something strange and altogether new.

- I understand that this loss is not the impetus you would have asked for, if it were a choice, to help you grow and change. Still, it may have brought bittersweet gifts into your life that you would not otherwise have—new support people, new routines, new attitudes, new perspectives, new hopes, or a new purpose.

- Many grieving parents emerge from the early years of grief as stronger, more anchored people. Perhaps you are more assertive and apt to say what you really believe. Maybe you wear fewer masks and can be more of your true self in the presence of others.

- What's more, you may have discovered the depths of your compassion for others, compassion you were unaware was a part of you. Don't be surprised if you find yourself volunteering, engaging in random acts of daily kindness, or being more emotionally and spiritually attuned to others.

CARPE DIEM
Take a moment to write down what kind of transformations
you have noticed in yourself since your miscarriage.
Have you also noticed that your partner is transforming,
and how do you feel about the transformations occurring?

A FINAL WORD

"But grief still has to be worked through. It is like walking through water. Sometimes there is an enormous breaker that knocks me down. Sometimes there is a sudden and fierce squall. But I know that many waters cannot quench love, neither can the floods drown it."

— Madeleine L'Engle

Early pregnancy is a time betwixt and between. So is grief. Grief is the experience that marks the threshold between presence and absence. It is the threshold that opens onto the rest of your life after loss.

There are two paths on the other side of that threshold. On one, you carry your grief inside, where it will live forever as locked-up pain and result in symptoms like ongoing depression and anxiety. On the other path, you express your grief openly and honestly so that you can heal. The choice is yours.

Grieving parents have taught me so much. They have taught me to slow down, to enjoy the moment, to find hidden treasures everywhere—a beautiful sunrise, a flower in bloom, a hike in the woods, a friend's gentle touch, a child's smile.

Grieving parents have taught me that there is so much to learn about ourselves and the world around us. They have taught me to live fully in the present while remembering our past and embracing our future.

Grieving parents have taught me to be open to giving and receiving love. They have taught me to seek a sense of belonging, a sense of meaning, a sense of purpose both in my life's work and in my relationships with family and friends. They have taught me there are magic and miracles in loving and being loved.

Most important, grieving parents have taught me so very much about what it means to yearn for and love a child. Their lessons have permeated my soul and my ways of being with my own children.

On your grief journey, I hope you choose the path of mourning. To mourn well is to live and love well again. Will you truly live or will you merely exist?

Choosing to mourn openly, honestly, and authentically is, ultimately, to choose life and to rediscover hope, which is an expectation of a good that is yet to be.

Choose hope. Choose to live. Godspeed.

RESOURCES

Angel Whispers Baby Loss Support Program
(www.angelwhispers.ca/angelwhispers)
Angel Whispers provides support and programs for parents who have lost a baby shortly after birth, during pregnancy, miscarriage, or stillbirth. They offer a quarterly newsletter as well as care packages and birth certificate keepsakes.

The Center for Loss in Multiple Birth (CLIMB), Inc.
(www.climb-support.org)
This site was developed by and for parents throughout the United States, Canada, and beyond who have experienced the death of one or more children during a multiple pregnancy, the birthing process, or in early infancy.

HAND: Helping After Neonatal Death (www.handonline.org)
HAND, which stands for Helping After Neonatal Death, is a nonprofit, volunteer group that provides support and information to bereaved parents, their families, and friends following a miscarriage, stillbirth, or newborn death.

Heavenly Angels in Need (www.heavenlyangelsinneed.com)
This agency provides burial items for babies as well as memory boxes free to grieving families.

Honored Babies (www.HonoredBabies.org)
A supportive site for parents whose babies have died due to miscarriage, ectopic pregnancy, stillbirth, neonatal death, infancy death, and/or pregnancy termination. On this site you will find online memorials, online support group email lists (there's also one for grandmothers), and a place to share your story.

Hygeia (www.hygeiafoundation.org)
Hygeia Foundation for Perinatal Loss and Bereavement, Inc.'s mission is to provide support during the painful experience of grief after the loss of a pregnancy or newborn child. Included are a resource center, poetry, memories and mementos, and stories.

Infants Remembered In Silence, Inc. (IRIS) (www.irisremembers.com)
IRIS was founded in 1987 and works with bereaved parents, families, and

friends who have had an early pregnancy death, stillbirth, neonatal death, or a child die from birth defects, illness, accidents, and all other forms of infant and/or early childhood death.

Father's Page (www.missfoundation.org/support/articles/dads)
From the MISS site, just for dads.

Missing GRACE Organization (www.missinggrace.org)
The Missing GRACE Organization helps families on their journey through pregnancy and infant loss, infertility, and adoption. Provides support and resources to aid parents as they grieve, restore, arise, commemorate, and educate.

Mommies Enduring Neonatal Death (www.mend.org)
M.E.N.D. is a Christian nonprofit whose purpose is to reach out to those who have lost a child due to miscarriage, stillbirth, or early infant death and offer a way to share experiences and information through meetings, a bi-monthly newsletter, and website.

A Place to Remember (www.aplacetoremember.com)
A site committed to publishing and providing support materials and resources for those who have been touched by a crisis in pregnancy or the death of a baby.

Remembered Forever (www.remembered-forever.org)
This site offers users the chance to create a personalized online memorial for their lost loved ones. You can add photos, memories, videos, tributes, and stories as well as light virtual candles in remembrance.

SPALS: Subsequent Pregnancy After Loss (www.spals.com)
SPALS is a warm and compassionate group of people who have experienced the loss of a child due to miscarriage, selective termination, stillbirth, neonatal death, sudden infant death, or accidental death.

THE MOURNER'S CODE

Ten Self-Compassionate Principles

Though you should reach out to others as you journey through grief, you should not feel obligated to accept the unhelpful responses you may receive from some people. You are the one who is grieving, and as such, you have certain "rights" no one should try to take away from you.

The following list is intended both to empower you to heal and to decide how others can and cannot help. This is not to discourage you from reaching out to others for help, but rather to assist you in distinguishing useful responses from hurtful ones.

1. **You have the right to experience your own unique grief.**
    No one else will grieve in exactly the same way you do. So, when you turn to others for help, don't allow them to tell you what you should or should not be feeling.

2. **You have the right to talk about your grief.**
    Talking about your grief will help you heal. Seek out others who will allow you to talk as much as you want, as often as you want, about your grief. If at times you don't feel like talking, you also have the right to be silent.

3. **You have the right to feel a multitude of emotions.**
    Confusion, numbness, disorientation, fear, guilt, and relief are just a few of the emotions you might feel as part of your grief journey. Others may try to tell you that feeling angry, for example, is wrong. Don't take these judgmental responses to heart. Instead, find listeners who will accept your feelings without condition.

4. **You have the right to be tolerant of your physical and emotional limits.**
    Your feelings of loss and sadness will probably leave you feeling fatigued. Respect what your body and mind are telling you. Get daily rest. Eat balanced meals. And don't allow others to push you into doing things you don't feel ready to do.

5. **You have the right to experience "griefbursts."**

   Sometimes, out of nowhere, a powerful surge of grief may overcome you. This can be frightening, but it is normal and natural. Find someone who understands and will let you talk it out.

6. **You have the right to make use of ritual.**

   Rituals and ceremonies after a loss help us acknowledge the reality and importance of the loss, express our thoughts and feelings, and bring together people who can support one another. If others tell you that funerals, memorial ceremonies, or other healing rituals such as these are silly or unnecessary, don't listen.

7. **You have the right to embrace your spirituality.**

   If faith is a part of your life, express it in ways that seem appropriate to you. Allow yourself to be around people who understand and support your religious beliefs. If you feel angry at God, find someone to talk with who won't be critical of your feelings of hurt and abandonment.

8. **You have the right to search for meaning.**

   You may find yourself asking, "Why did this miscarriage have to happen? Why me? Why now?" Some of your questions may have answers, but some may not. And watch out for the clichéd responses some people may give you. Comments like, "It was God's will" or "Think of what you have to be thankful for" are not helpful and you do not have to accept them.

9. **You have the right to treasure your memories.**

   Memories are one of the best legacies that exist after loss. You will always remember. Instead of ignoring your memories, find others with whom you can share them.

10. **You have the right to move toward your grief and heal.**

    Reconciling your grief will not happen quickly. Remember, grief is a process, not an event. Be patient and tolerant with yourself and avoid people who are impatient and intolerant with you. Neither you nor those around you must forget that pregnancy loss changes your life forever.

ALSO BY ALAN WOLFELT

The Depression of Grief
Coping with Your Sadness and Knowing When to Get Help

When someone you love dies, it's normal and necessary to grieve. Grief is the thoughts and feelings you have inside you, and sadness is often the most prominent and painful emotion. In other words, it's normal to be depressed after a loss. This compassionate guide will help you understand your natural depression, express it in ways that will help you heal, and know when you may be experiencing a more severe or clinical depression that would be eased by professional treatment. A section for caregivers that explores the new DSM-5 criteria for Major Depression is also included.

"This enlightening book revealed to me that I am not flawed and it further gave me the strength to go back and do a bit more work so I could truly mourn the loss of my mom and start living life once again."
— Kerry Bratton

"This is a much needed resource for both persons who are experiencing grief and professional caregivers who often have a limited understanding of the subtle differences between grief and clinical depression. This book is not only thorough and informative; it is written in a way that is relevant to any person involved in grief and bereavement work."
— Jane Castle

ISBN 978-1-61722-193-4 • 128 pages • softcover • $14.95

Companion
PRESS

All Dr. Wolfelt's publications can be ordered by mail from:
Companion Press
3735 Broken Bow Road
Fort Collins, CO 80526
(970) 226-6050
www.centerforloss.com

ALSO BY ALAN WOLFELT

Healing Your Grieving Heart After Stillbirth
100 Practical Ideas for Parents and Families

by Alan D. Wolfelt, Ph.D. and Raelynn Maloney, Ph.D.

The stillbirth of a hoped-for child is an inexplicable loss of hopes and dreams of a new life—to the parents, to the siblings this baby may have, to the extended family, and to friends. The impact of this overwhelming loss is profound and life-changing.

This compassionate guide contains 100 practical ideas to help those affected by the tragedy of stillbirth. Some of the ideas teach about the principles of grief and mourning. Others offer practical, action-oriented tips for coping with the natural difficulties of this loss, such as communication between spouses, explaining the death to others, reconciling anger or guilt, remembering the baby who died, and many others.

ISBN 978-1-61722-175-0 • 128 pages • softcover • $11.95

Companion
PRESS

All Dr. Wolfelt's publications can be ordered by mail from:
Companion Press
3735 Broken Bow Road
Fort Collins, CO 80526
(970) 226-6050
www.centerforloss.com

ALSO BY ALAN WOLFELT

Finding the Words
How to Talk to Children and Teens about Death, Suicide, Funerals, Homicide, Cremation, and Other End-of-Life Matters

It's hard to talk to children and teens about death and dying, particularly when someone they love has died or might die soon. Our instinct as caring adults may be to shelter them from painful truths. Yet, as Dr. Wolfelt emphasizes, what kids need most is our honesty and our loving presence.

This practical and compassionate handbook includes dozens of suggested phrases to use with preschoolers, school-agers, and teenagers as you explain death in general or the death of a parent, a sibling, a grandparent, or a pet. Other chapters include possible words and ideas to draw on when you are talking to kids about a death by suicide, homicide, or terminal illness. At times, grown-ups must also have very difficult conversations with dying children; this book offers guidance. A final chapter discusses how to talk with kids about funerals, burial, and cremation.

ISBN 978-1-61722-189-7 • 144 pages • softcover • $14.95

Companion
PRESS

All Dr. Wolfelt's publications can be ordered by mail from:
Companion Press
3735 Broken Bow Road
Fort Collins, CO 80526
(970) 226-6050
www.centerforloss.com

TRAINING AND SPEAKING ENGAGEMENTS

To contact Dr. Wolfelt about speaking engagements or
training opportunities at his Center for Loss and Life Transition,
email him at DrWolfelt@centerforloss.com